WARRIORS,
GODS & SPIRITS
from
CENTRAL & SOUTH
AMERICAN MYTHOLOGY

WARRIORS, GODS & SPIRITS
from
CENTRAL & SOUTH AMERICAN MYTHOLOGY

TEXT BY DOUGLAS GIFFORD
ILLUSTRATIONS BY JOHN SIBBICK

SCHOCKEN BOOKS
NEW YORK

DOUGLAS & McINTYRE
VANCOUVER/TORONTO

Copyright © 1983
by Eurobook Limited
Published by Agreement with
Eurobook Limited, London

First American edition published
by Schocken Books 1983
10 9 8 7 6 5 4 3 2 1   82 83 84 85 86 87

**Library of Congress Cataloging
in Publication Data**
Gifford, Douglas.
    Warriors, gods & spirits from
Central and South American
mythology
    (World mythologies series)
    Includes index.
    1. Indians—Religion   and
mythology.   2.   Indians—
Legends. I. Sibbick, John. II.
Title. III. Series.
E59.R38G53   1983   299′.7928
82–25185

Published in Canada by
Douglas & McIntyre Ltd.
1615 Venables Street
Vancouver, British Columbia

**Canadian   Cataloguing   in
Publication Data**
Gifford, Douglas.
    Warriors, gods & spirits from
Central and South American
mythology
    (World mythologies)
    Includes index
    ISBN 0-88894-386-5
    1. Indians of Central America
— Legends — Juvenile literature. 2. Indians of South
America — Legends — Juvenile   literature.   I. Sibbick,
John. II. Title III. Series.
PZ8.1.G53Wa   j398.2′098
C83-091062-X

Printed in Great Britain by
William Collins, Glasgow
ISBN 0-8052-3857-3 (Schocken)
ISSN 0732-2291

ISBN 0-88894-386-5 (Douglas & McIntyre)

Contents

Myths of the New World

The continent of Central and South America stretches from north of the Equator to the cold south Atlantic waters and contains many different types of environment. Along its western side are the Andes mountains, part of a fold in the earth's surface which runs from Alaska to Tierra del Fuego. Many of the mountains are active volcanoes and while their lower slopes and valleys are often thickly forested, their highest peaks are snow-covered all year round. To the east of the mountains lie the tropical forests of the great river basins of the Amazon and Orinoco and the hot plateau lands of southern Brazil and eastern Bolivia. Further south is the dry scrub jungle of the Gran Chaco and the pampas, the rolling grasslands of Uruguay and Argentina. Coastal deserts, high, cold plateaux and the stormy coastlands at the extreme tip of the continent add to the region's immense variety.

Like the Indians of North America, the original inhabitants of South and Central America probably came from Asia some 25,000 years ago and they finally reached and colonized the cold southern lands about 10,000 years ago. When the first Europeans arrived at the beginning of the sixteenth century, they found a whole range of life styles well established. The forest and river people, living close to nature and having a deep understanding of their environment, seemed remote to the city-based invaders and were therefore labelled primitive. The peoples of the mountain plateaux, the Aztecs, Mayas and Incas, who had built great cities and empires, seemed far more advanced. Eager for the gold, silver and precious stones they saw around them, the Europeans conquered and enslaved the Indians. More peaceful settlers soon followed to farm the land and exploit the riches of the forests; later, African slaves were brought in as servants and labourers. In some areas the settlers lived peacefully with the Indians but in others the Indian tribes were largely destroyed, either by deliberate persecution or by European diseases against which they had no immunity.

From this mixture of tribes and races, the stories spill out like treasure from a vast chest of drawers. There is the Indian drawer, which itself contains a great variety of tales in different languages and from different cultures. There is the European drawer, with stories told by the settlers who came from Spain, Italy, Portugal, Germany, France,

Britain and many other countries. And there are drawers containing tales which are mixtures of Indian and European or of Indian and African sources.

The stories in this book come mainly from Indian sources and fall into three basic categories. First, there are the legends which tell of the Aztec, Maya and Inca empires and which were written down as history rather than as myths. We know these mainly from the records of the sixteenth- and seventeenth-century Spanish and Portuguese chroniclers who, although they disapproved of what they regarded as devilish ideas, did pass on what the peoples themselves believed to be their history. Second come the myths collected in modern times by more scientific and less prejudiced methods. These deal not so much with gods and emperors as with the origins of everyday things such as fire, coca or honey. They reveal an intimate understanding of the forest and the river and a desire to know how to live with nature rather than how to conquer or control it. Thirdly, there are legends and myths which come from either the first or the second type but which have been influenced by non-Indian ways of thought or storytelling. Mixing of myths from different cultures occurs whenever peoples intermingle and these stories are no less interesting and authentic than the first two types. We can be sure that even the so-called 'pure' myths and stories are actually a mixture of more than one tradition. The Aztecs, for example, took over many legends from their predecessors, the Toltecs, and made them their own; the Incas adopted the gods and traditions of the people they conquered; one jungle tribe fights another and takes the best of its defeated enemy's stories as its own. Mixing of Indian and non-Indian themes and styles is a continuation of a process as old as story-telling itself.

Legends and myths often have an underlying purpose and the actions of gods and heroes are influenced by ideas of good conduct or accepted practice. The heroes and villains of the stories represent different qualities and bring abstract concepts to life in a way that people can easily understand. Their adventures represent the ideals, worries and problems of ordinary human beings; the whole canvas of legend and myth,

though it includes historical events, is in the end, a picture of the human mind itself.

Many of the tales from every part of the region have animal heroes and the first thing we notice is that these usually have recognizably human characteristics, both good and bad. Frogs can be skilled hunters; foxes and rabbits are usually clever and cunning; jaguars are powerful but not always very intelligent. Often animals were given god-like status, because people believed gods were originally in animal form. The unseen spirits represented by the animals were adopted as totems, or objects of especial significance, by different tribes. In a tribe whose totem or god-figure is a frog, for instance, the spirit doctor or shaman will dress up as a frog, make a noise like a frog, in fact be to all intents and purposes a frog while he is performing his tribe's sacred ceremonies. In another tribe a shaman may have his body painted with spots so that he looks like a jaguar. Even when the actual idea of the totem is forgotten by the tribe, the animals that were the original totem figures remain very much alive in the myths.

Another important concept which pervades all Indian thought is the idea of animism, which attributes a living soul to inanimate objects, plants and other natural things. Clouds, stones or earthenware figures may be seen as gods not only because they stand for a supernatural being but because they actually look like what they represent. This idea of becoming what you resemble is also applied to human beings, particularly to the shamans, the spiritual leaders of the tribe. When the shaman paints his body to make himself look like a jaguar, he feels that he receives the jaguar's living soul and, with it, the animal's supernatural powers. To him and to the onlookers his ordinary human nature seems to die and, reborn as a jaguar, he is able to help his people.

This myth of rebirth into a new, spiritual form, occurs again and again throughout the myths of Central and South America, from the sophisticated versions of Aztec and Inca legend to beliefs still held today by the survivors of the forest tribes. In the end, the pattern behind the Indian's thought does not change very much over the centuries.

12

Gods of the Aztecs

Good land has always attracted settlers and the Valley of Mexico is no exception. It is a natural basin set in a range of mountains and volcanoes, measuring some 3,000 square miles and lying between 2,100 and 2,400 metres above sea level. Once covered by a shallow lake, it was the centre of a succession of Indian civilizations which dated back to around 2000 BC. It was here, in 1519, that the Spanish conquistadores came upon the great Aztec empire, a highly organized society with practical and artistic skills which amazed and impressed the travellers.

The most important of the older civilizations was that of the Olmecs (800 to 400 BC) but of more direct influence on the Aztecs was the great civilization known as the Classic Age which had its centre in Teotihuacan and lasted from around AD 300 to 600. Teotihuacan itself was a great city whose temples and huge pyramids of the Sun and Moon remain to this day. It governed most of the tribes of the central highlands of Mexico in what seems to have been an age of peace and prosperity, for no fortifications have been found and there is no evidence of wars from this time. Some of the gods worshipped by the people of Teotihuacan were known also to the Aztecs—the Feathered Serpent (later known as Quetzalcoatl), the Sun and Rain gods; but there was no trace of the fierce war gods nor of the human sacrifices which were a feature of Aztec religion. Around AD 600 some disaster occurred—perhaps an invasion or some economic failure—and Teotihuacan's power came to an end.

The second civilization to influence the Aztecs was that of the Toltecs, whose capital was at Tula (Tollan). By AD 980 they had taken over the administration of many of the tribes in the area and their influence spread even outside the Valley of Mexico, to the cultures of the Mixtecs and Zapotecs. The Toltecs were skilled builders and understood metal-working as well as pottery and weaving. Their history as told by the Aztecs was rather different from what archaeologists now believe to be the true facts. In reality the Toltecs seem to have been a grim, warlike race who suppressed their opponents ruthlessly. The Aztecs, however, identified their leader Tialtzin with the Feathered Serpent god Quetzalcoatl and saw him as a peace-loving man and a gentle ruler. According to Aztec tradition and legend,

HUITZILOPOCHTLI

TLÁLOC

XIUTECUTLI

Quetzalcoatl/Tialtzin was challenged by a warlike faction who had as their tribal god the fierce Tezcatlipoca (the Smoking Mirror). The fight between the two groups, which is told as a struggle between the gods themselves, brought an end to the power of Tollan and the Toltecs.

Whatever the true cause of its downfall, the Toltec empire ended between 1156 and 1168. To the west, the cultures of the Zapotecs and Mixtecs continued to flourish. The Zapotecs lived near the modern town of Oaxaca and the remains of their great temple pyramids still stand on the flat-topped mountain ridge of Monte Alban. They were apparently skilled metal workers and potters and were the builders of Mitla, 'the place of the dead', where chiefs were buried in imposing tombs and where a great stone temple stood, its walls painted with frescoes and decorated with intricate mosaics. The Mixtecs, whose history can be traced back to AD 692, lived between Pueblo and Oaxaca. Among the articles that have been preserved from their times are vividly painted books made of folded bark paper or deerskin.

After the fall of the Toltecs, several small city states ruled in the Valley of Mexico. The last group of people to arrive in the area were the Aztecs themselves, whose name means 'people whose face nobody knows'. They came from the north-west, bringing with them their tribal war god Huitzilopochtli and a tradition of human sacrifice to appease him. They were fierce fighters and soon acquired a reputation as useful mercenaries but there is little doubt that they were looked on as barbaric and uncivilized by the gentler city states of the Valley. For a long time the Aztecs lived as scavengers, working as labourers where they could, raiding villages and townships and carrying off both goods and women. They were often thrown out of their settlements by enraged farmers and townspeople used to more civilized behaviour.

Eventually they settled on two swampy islands in the Valley's great lake and in about 1320 they founded the city of Tenochtitlan, a city which was later to be the centre of their empire.

While the Aztecs had been a wandering tribe they had gradually acquired the culture of the city states for which they worked, absorbing their language, traditions and gods. When they grew strong and began to conquer their former masters, they saw themselves as inheritors of the great Toltec culture and, by the simple expedient of rewriting their history, they came to consider themselves as the actual descendants of the Toltecs, with the age of Tollan as a kind of golden age of peace and prosperity.

By 1500 the Aztecs had conquered a very large area of central Mexico and established a powerful social and political system. They used a kind of picture writing, had their own mathematical system and relied on a complex calendar for calculating the days and months. Their language, Nahuatl, was common to many of the Valley tribes—and is today the principal indigenous language of Mexico.

Aztec religion was a fusion of the beliefs of many tribes, with gods and goddesses ruling over different aspects of life. Among the principal gods were Tlaloc, the Rain god, to whom children were sacrificed; Xiutecutli, the Fire god and Lord of all Volcanoes; Huitzilopochtli, god of War and of the Sun; the Feathered Serpent Quetzalcoatl and his great rival Tezcatlipoca, who is identified with night and the dead as well as with sorcery and magic. Mictlantecutli, the Lord of the Underworld, ruled over Mictlan, the kingdom of the dead. For most souls, the path after death led through a succession of stages to the ninth hell, the eternal house of the dead. Some more fortunate beings ended up in a heavenly paradise with the Rain god while warriors who died in battle, those who were sacrificed and women who died in childbirth, found a new life in the Sun's domain.

The Aztec empire came to an end in 1521 after two years of struggle against the Spanish invaders. The last emperor, Montezuma II, was more a philosopher than a warrior king and lived in far greater splendour and luxury than his predecessors. His brave fighters were ill equipped to meet the conquistadores, who had both horses and guns and in spite of some early successes, the Aztecs were eventually defeated. Montezuma himself, however, was not forgotten. His name, like those of the rulers of Tollan before him, passed into legend and he, too, became part of the mythology of the Indians of Mexico.

The five Suns

According to Aztec tradition, the history of the world was made up of five Ages, or five Suns. There are many different versions of the legend of the Suns. Some say that the first Age took place in a world full of darkness and that there were only animals ranging about in the gloomy parts where any life could survive. If humans were born they were immediately devoured by wild cats or ocelots. So powerful were these animals that the time was also known as the Age of the Wild Cat. After a time some people did survive because the ocelots could not eat them all but when the Age of Wild Cats ended the men who remained turned into monkeys.

Most of the traditions agree that the first four Suns were called after the four elements: earth, air, fire and water, though some include an Age of Famine. During each Sun Age, living beings were created but each Age ended in catastrophe. The Earth Sun, which some say was also the Age of Giants, ended with violent earthquakes, when whole mountains toppled into the sea. The Fire Sun ended with a rain of molten lava, with raging fires that burned up all the land. The only living things to survive this terror were the birds and some people who were able to turn into birds themselves and fly out of danger. The Air Sun ended with hurricanes and whirlwinds which swept away trees, buildings, even towering rocks and cliffs. The Water Sun ended with a great flood which drowned all living creatures except the fish and two human beings, Tata and Nena.

Tata and Nena were working in the fields one day when the Water Sun sent for them.
'I am going to send a great flood to cover the earth,' he said, 'and I shall drown everyone in it. But you shall be saved.'
'How shall we escape when you send the water, O sacred Water Sun?' asked Nena.
'You must find a strong tree in the middle of the forest,' said the Water Sun, 'and make a hole in it, just as if you were a tree-climbing monkey who is trying to hide. Make sure the hole is high above the ground, at the top of the tree. Then get in and stay there until the waters have passed. But remember, when you come down to the earth again, you must not be greedy and take more than you need. You may have one corn cob each and no more.'

The man and woman hurried off and found the biggest tree in the middle of the forest, a fine old tree which was hundreds of years old and seemed to reach the sky. They clambered up its thick trunk and, among the branches of its canopy, found a place where the tree was already hollow. There was plenty of room for them both and they settled themselves in comfortably to wait.

So the waters came and the flood rose higher and higher, carrying everything with it as it swirled along. Tata and Nena stayed securely in their hole in the tree and watched it all: the floating branches, the trees torn up by the roots, the cooking pots and the tools from the farms, the animals and people swept along in the water.

After what seemed a very long time indeed the waters subsided and the two humans crawled out of their hole in the tree and carefully climbed down the great trunk which had stood firmly rooted in the earth. By now they were longing for something to eat and when they saw a fish swimming by in a stream which was still swollen with the flood, they completely forgot the Water Sun's orders.

'Come, let's take it,' said Tata and they caught the fish, built a fire of sticks and began to cook it. The smoke from the fire wound up through the branches of the forest trees, a thin trail rising straight into the sky. The Water Sun saw the smoke and peered down to see what they were cooking.

'Why did you disobey me?' he thundered. 'I told you to eat only a corn cob each.'

Taking a great stick he struck them both on the head, removing the part of their brains that made humans like the gods and changing them into dogs. The Age of the Water Sun was over.

The Fifth Sun was born at Teotihuacan, the holy city where the great Pyramid of the Sun was to be constructed. The Fifth Sun brought together all four elements, and is the Age in which we are now living. Some say it is the Age of Earthquakes, Famine, War and Confusion; others that under the Fifth Sun the world will survive because the four warring elements are balanced together. But, said the Aztecs, the balance can only be kept if the chief being, Man, continually strives towards perfection through penance and sacrifice.

The new Sun

After the Age of the Fourth Sun had ended, there was nothing to light up the world. Without light nothing could grow. Plants could not flower, humans could not live, animals could not see to follow their paths through the forests. The gods met together to discuss what should be done. Finally a small god whose skin was covered in scabs and spots, and whom no-one thought much of, was appointed to give light to the world. 'You, Nanahuatzin, you must take it upon yourself to find light, to create the Sun, to bring the warmth that keeps life in man,' they said.

Nanahuatzin accepted humbly but at the same time another rather boastful god also offered to help, hoping to win praise and glory for himself. His name was Teccuciztecatl, the sea-shell god.

Before such an important event as providing a new Sun, even gods must prepare themselves and Nanahuatzin and Teccuciztecatl spent four days fasting and doing penance for their past misdeeds.

In this way they would be fully freed from any ill-feelings which might affect what they were to create. After they had fasted, the two gods lit a fire and made offerings before it. The offerings of Teccuciztecatl were magnificent. There were beautifully worked flints, brilliant feathers from sacred birds, precious stones and nuggets of gold. Poor Nanahuatzin had only very humble objects to offer but he gave what he could: green fronds of grass and reeds, tied in bundles of three, thorns stained with his own blood, even the scabs off his own pimples. All the gods laughed to see such a contrast and agreed that of the two, the god Teccuciztecatl's offerings were by far the more impressive.

The time came for the ceremony to begin and just at midnight, when the dark world was at its very darkest, the two gods came before a great fire. Teccuciztecatl was beautifully dressed in rich robes; Nanahuatzin wore a kind of papery cloth made from tree bark. Their task was to sacrifice themselves and so create the Sun which was to give light to the world.

Teccuciztecatl approached the fire first but as soon as he felt its searing heat he shrank back. Again he walked towards it and again he drew back. Four times he tried but still he could not bring himself to throw himself into the flames. Then Nanahuatzin, small and humble as he was, simply walked straight up to the fire and disappeared into its centre. Only then was Teccuciztecatl so ashamed that he rushed headlong after him.

As the gods stood praising Nanahuatzin's courage, a great light spread in the sky and the little pimply god emerged from the fire as the Sun itself. Shortly afterwards, Teccuciztecatl also appeared as the Moon, shining as brightly, then, as the Sun. The gods laughed to see the boastful god who had been shamed into throwing himself on the fire and they threw a rabbit up at him to dim his light to a pale reflection of the Sun's. To this day, marks in the shape of a rabbit can be seen on the Moon's face.

The new Sun and Moon were without motion and in order to set them swinging on their heavenly courses, the other gods decided that they, too, must sacrifice themselves. One by one they threw themselves into the fire. All, that is,

Myths of creation

The stories the Aztec people told about the creation of the world start with a formless universe where nothing is alive except the gods. There is no light; everything is dark. One story tells how among the gods were a prince, his beloved wife and their child. The family were living in a cave and there, sadly, the child died. The parents buried it carefully in the ground and from his hair grew cotton, from his ears the seed-bearing plants, from his nostrils a sweet-scented herb which cools fever, from his fingers the sweet potato and from his finger nails, maize.

Food was now available for man and he soon appeared, but though he had all the plants and fruits of the earth, he still felt nothing towards his fellow men and thought of nothing except his day-to-day survival.

Another story tells how the vine first came to the earth. The wind god Ehecatl, a form of the great god Quetzalcoatl, fell in love with a girl called Mayahuel, who lived in the home of the gods under the guardianship of an old woman called Tzitzimil. Ehecatl visited her one day while the household was asleep. He quietly awoke her and they stole away secretly, without disturbing the guardian. They travelled down to earth and as soon as their feet touched the ground they grew together into a great tree with two strong branches, one belonging to the wind god and one to Mayahuel. Ehecatl's branch soon produced fresh green leaves but a little while later Mayahuel's was covered in delicate flowers.

When the guardian Tzitzimil awoke she was furious at losing a girl who had been in her care and, with a troop of young gods, she rushed down to earth to punish the runaways. She was very determined and it was not long before she found the tree and recognized the character of Mayahuel in the flowering branch. In her rage she called on lightning to strike the tree and split the two branches from each other. Snatching Mayahuel's branch she tore it to pieces and handed them to the young gods, who scattered them on the ground, tearing at them with their teeth, gnawing them into fragments. The branch which belonged

except the god called Xolotl, twin to the great Quetzalcoatl himself. He was so frightened that he changed himself from one shape to another until he was finally captured and thrown into the flames. When he emerged, Xolotl had become the god of magic and magicians, able to change into any shape he chose. Still the Sun and Moon hung motionless in the sky so Quetzalcoatl summoned a great wind which blew with such violence that first the Sun, then the Moon, were forced before it across the sky. So the Age of the Fifth Sun began.

The idea of sacrifice was an important part of Aztec religion but the human sacrifices which so revolted the first European visitors to the Aztecs were not always those of captives and slaves. In the great spring festival of the god Tezcatlipoca, a single youth, chosen the previous year, may originally have been a willing victim.

For most of the year the boy was treated with great honour, dressed in the finest clothes, trained to sing and play the flute and served by eight pages who went with him everywhere. He was considered to be himself a god. Twenty days before the festival, he was dressed as an Aztec chief and given four beautiful women as his wives. For five days before the sacrifice, there was continual feasting and dancing. On the last day he and his wives left the city but the wives abandoned him before he reached the temple where the final rites took place. As he ascended the four steps, he broke a flute on each level. On the stone altar, the priests killed him with a single blow from a stone knife and presented his heart to the Sun. A new youth was chosen at once to take his place, to be honoured as the reborn god, and to be sacrificed in his turn the following year.

to Ehecatl remained untouched on the tree.

When Tzitzimil and her young gods had returned to the home of the gods, the wind god Ehecatl resumed his normal form. Sadly he walked over the ground where the gods had scattered the fragments of Mayahuel's branch. As he mourned the loss of his love, he saw that the pieces of wood had turned into bone and he buried them carefully in the field. From these bones sprang the first shoots of the vine, flowering as Mayahuel's branch had flowered and producing the sweet grapes from which men learned to make wine.

Both these myths are concerned with the plants of the earth but another, more sinister story involves not only creation, but also the Aztec tradition of human sacrifice.

It is said that at the beginning of time there was only water. In the water swam a monster with many mouths. The gods Quetzalcoatl and Tezcatlipoca decided that this monstrous creature should provide form for the universe, which was then quite without shape of any kind. The two gods took hold of the monster. One held its right foreleg and back left leg, the other its left foreleg and right back leg and they struggled with it day and night until it was defeated. When it was exhausted and could fight no more, the two gods tore the monster into two pieces. From the lower part they formed the heavens and from the upper part the earth. Its hair provided the grass and trees, flowers came from its skin, caves and wells from its eyes, mountains and valleys from its nose.

At night, the great Earth Monster could be heard howling, starving and hungry, crying out for human hearts to eat and human blood to drink. To provide for it, constant sacrifices had to be made and enemies of the Aztecs were killed to feed it with the blood it craved.

Yet another story was told to explain the social structure of the Aztecs and the existence of the warrior class which dominated Aztec society before the Spanish conquest.

In the old days there were two gods, Ometeotl and his wife Omecihuatl. One day Omecihuatl gave birth not to a child but to a stone knife which she threw from heaven down to the earth below. Immediately sixteen hundred warriors sprang up

from the earth, each one a man of great valour and strength. Being proud men, however, and being quite alone on the earth, they asked their mother to create a race of serving men who would look after them.

'Your thoughts are not the thoughts of noble men,' replied Omecihuatl, 'but of arrogant and selfish warriors who think of nothing but their own desires. Come! Think again and see if you cannot have wiser ideas than this. Isn't there more to life than satisfying your hunger and thirst? A place with the gods is yours if you can only raise your thoughts above the earth.'

'That's no use to us,' said the warrior leaders. 'Soldiers are rough men, we can't discuss religion and philosophy. We love this earth: we love the vine and what it gives us; we love the food and we love the sun. All we need now is servants to look after us and bring us food and drink when it is due.'

Omecihuatl would not listen, so the sixteen hundred warriors turned instead to the God of the Underworld, Mictlantecutli, who sat brooding in the darkness of Mictlan, the kingdom below the earth.

'Listen to us,' said the warriors. 'Many men have died in disasters over the last Ages—there have been floods and terrible fires, thunderbolts and lightning, hurricanes and whirlwinds, earthquakes and famines. Have you any ashes of the dead or even bones that we could have?'

Although they did not say so, the warriors hoped that if they poured their own blood over a bone or a heap of human ashes, it would bring the remains to life once more. In this way they could create a man and a woman who would repopulate the whole earth and provide them with a race of people to be their servants.

'Send me a man who can carry such a bone,' said the God of the Underworld.

None of the heroes was strong enough to enter the Kingdom of Mictlan but they called on Xolotl, god of Magic and twin brother of Quetzalcoatl, to undertake the task for them.

It was dark and smoky in the region of the dead, like the inside of a volcano. Cautiously, Xolotl approached Mictlantecutli and his wife Mictlancihuatl, who ruled over the spirits of the dead in the nine realms of the Aztec hell.

'I have come to carry the bones of man to the earth above,' he said.

'What you want is dangerous,' said Mictlantecutli seriously. 'These men were destroyed because they angered the gods before. Will you risk that happening again?'

'The risk is ours,' said Xolotl persuasively. 'Give me the bones.'

The God of the Underworld held out a bone to him and, quick as lightning, the God of Magic took it from him and began to run as fast as he could along the stony path that led back to earth. 'Give me back the bone,' called Mictlantecutli, changing his mind; but it was too late.

As Xolotl ran, however, he could not see where he was going and he tripped and fell in the darkness. The precious bone crashed to the ground and split into two parts, one big and one smaller. Xolotl gathered them both up and continued, stumbling now and then, but using his magic skills to escape the anger of Mictlantecutli. At last he reached the place where the sixteen hundred warriors were feasting.

'I've done it,' he gasped. 'Here are the bones.'

The warriors gathered round and one by one cut their arms with their daggers and poured a few drops of their own blood onto the pieces of bone.

A few days later a male child grew from the larger piece of bone and some days after that, a female grew from the smaller piece. The warriors nourished the children carefully on the milk of a thistle plant and in no time at all they had grown to their full height. As the warriors had planned, these reborn humans became their servants and, in time, their children and grandchildren became servants of the generations of warriors to come.

The story of Quetzalcoatl

Quetzalcoatl, the Feathered Serpent, was probably the most significant of all the Aztec gods. In his many forms he was a sky and sun god, god of the winds, the morning star and the benefactor of mankind. His name comes from *quetzal*, a rare bird with strikingly long green tail feathers, and *coatl*, which means snake. Under different names he was honoured throughout Mexico and Central America and the highest pyramid temple in Mexico, at his sacred city of Cholula, was dedicated to him, as was a circular temple in the great court of Tenochtitlan.

Quetzalcoatl was the son of the earth goddess Coatlicue. She was out one day on a hillside, performing acts of penance with her sisters, when a white feather floated down from the sky towards her. Gathering it up, she placed it next to her breast and in this way became pregnant. In due course her son was born.

Quetzalcoatl grew up into a good and gentle child who was so kind-hearted that he could scarcely bear to pick a flower for fear of hurting it. When he was urged to perform sacrifices, he refused, offering only bread, flowers and scents. He treated himself more harshly, however, and did penance by pricking his skin with cactus thorns until the blood ran.

As he grew older he discovered many secrets and skills which he passed on to mankind. He found where maize was hidden, he knew the value of precious stones, of gold and silver, of coloured shells and feathers and the uses of different plants.

Quetzalcoatl's goodness and purity angered the great god Tezcatlipoca, the Smoking Mirror. Tezcatlipoca was in many ways the opposite of Quetzalcoatl. It was said that he was so light, so quick, that he descended from the sky on a rope made from spiders' webs. He was a god of merriment but also of sorcery and discord, of prosperity and of destruction, an unpredictable trickster who brought life to man but demanded sacrifices and death to sustain him.

One day Tezcatlipoca came to Quetzalcoatl and held a mirror up so that he could see his reflection in it. To Quetzalcoatl's horror, what he saw was the wrinkled face of an old man, with sad sunken eyes. Fearing that he would be spurned by his people if they saw him like this, he covered his face and ran into hiding. Tezcatlipoca followed him to his retreat and persuaded him to look in the mirror once more. This time, however, he dressed him in a rich robe made of quetzal feathers and gave him a blue serpent mask made of finest turquoise. Reassured, Quetzalcoatl returned to his people.

Tezcatlipoca was not satisfied simply with demonstrating his power; he wanted to destroy

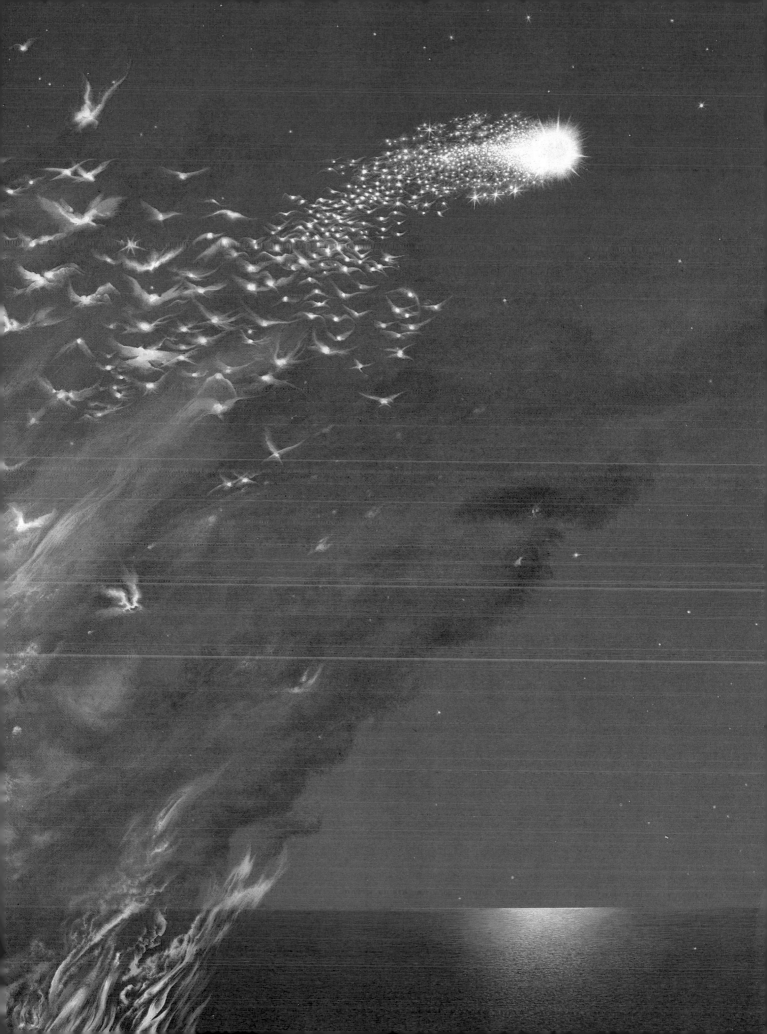

Quetzalcoatl's purity completely. Pretending to be friendly, he offered Quetzalcoatl a cup of pulque, a kind of wine made from the fermented sap of the agave plant. At first Quetzalcoatl refused but after a while he was persuaded to dip his finger into the cup and taste the wine. The first taste led to a sip, then to another and another and soon he was drinking eagerly. Growing merry, he called his sister to join him and they continued drinking together until both were quite intoxicated. Hardly knowing what they were doing, they fell into one another's arms and made love.

For a while Quetzalcoatl and his sister lived a life of drunken pleasure, abandoning their lives of purity and forgetting to perform their religious rites. Eventually, however, their heads cleared and they realized the enormity of what they had done. Overcome with guilt, Quetzalcoatl ordered his servants to build a stone coffin and in this he lay for four days and nights in penance. Then he ordered his people to follow him to the sea-shore. There he built a great funeral pyre and, dressing himself once more in the quetzal feather robe and turquoise serpent mask, he flung himself into the flames.

The great fire burned all night and as dawn came, the body of Quetzalcoatl turned to ashes which spiralled out of the flames in the form of a great flock of birds. As the servants stood helplessly watching their god leave them forever, they noticed a new star gleaming strongly in the morning sky: Quetzalcoatl's heart had become the morning star.

The Aztecs worshipped Quetzalcoatl as a god but there are other tales about him which show that they also thought of him as a historical character. In these he is the wise ruler of Tollan, the chief city of the Toltec empire, which ended around 1160 AD. Nine Toltec kings took the name of Quetzalcoatl and it is quite possible that the legends grew up around a real person. There was also a strong tradition that he had come from a distant land.

The days when Quetzalcoatl ruled in Tollan were times of peace and prosperity. There was plenty of food for everyone, cotton grew in different colours in the fields and there were gold, silver and precious stones. The people of Tollan were skilled craftsmen and the city thrived. There came a time, however, when Quetzalcoatl grew old and his people grew lazy. Tezcatlipoca, his enemy, saw that it was time for him to act, and to force Quetzalcoatl from his land.

Disguising himself an an old, white-headed man, Tezcatlipoca presented himself at Quetzalcoatl's palace and demanded to see the king.
'Your king is ill,' he told the guards, 'and I have medicine which will cure him. Take me to him.'

Tezcatlipoca was admitted and offered Quetzalcoatl a strong drug. Quetzalcoatl recognized the old man as a sign that his life was coming to an end and he asked where he should go.
'You must go to Tollantlapan,' said Tezcatlipoca. 'There you will find an old man waiting for you and he will transform you into a beautiful youth once more. Here, take this drink and you will understand everything.'

Though Quetzalcoatl was sick and old, he was not deceived. He accepted the medicine but refused to leave Tollan and Tezcatlipoca had to resort to another trick. Disguising himself as a seller of green chillies, he stood in the market place outside the palace until he attracted the attention of Quetzalcoatl's daughter. She had been carefully brought up, with little contact with strangers, and as soon as she saw this handsome young man she fell violently and passionately in love with him. Quite ill with love, she confessed to her father that the only man she would ever marry was the green chilli seller. If she could not marry him, she would die.

When Quetzalcoatl sent for the young man he could not at first be found, but just as the messengers were abandoning their search, he reappeared, as if by magic, in the market place and was brought to the palace. Reluctantly, Quetzalcoatl accepted him as his son-in-law and Tezcatlipoca became a powerful influence in the court.

Not surprisingly, the marriage of the green chilli seller to Quetzalcoatl's daughter caused jealousy and resentment among the Toltec people and, partly to distract their attention, Quetzalcoatl attacked a neighbouring tribe. The Toltecs saw their chance to destroy the young man but though they led him into the most dangerous positions, he fought bravely and returned home in triumph, more secure in his position than ever.

The green chilli seller now began to exert a hypnotic power over the Toltec people. First, he summoned them to a great festival, inviting people from far and near to attend. When the crowd was assembled, he began to sing and beat on a drum, urging them to sing with him and to follow as he danced. Following the steady rhythm of the drum, they danced like dreamers as he led them towards a deep ravine. Faster and faster went the drum, faster and faster went the dancing feet until, half mad with the music, they lost their balance on the narrow bridge and plunged to the valley below, to be turned into stones.

Next, he attacked a crowd working in Quetzalcoatl's flower garden, leaving hundreds dead among the flowers and on another occasion he turned himself into a sorcerer and attracted such a large gathering of people that many were crushed to death.

One disaster followed another until the Toltecs knew that the end of their empire was near. Finally, he caused all the food in Tollan to rot and, disguised as an old woman, began to roast a supply of fresh maize. The smell of good food attracted the remaining Toltecs to the old woman's house and there Tezcatlipoca destroyed them all.

Now Quetzalcoatl knew that the time had finally come for him to leave. Wearily he set fire to the city he had built, burying his gold and silver in the mountain valleys, changing cacao trees into worthless cacti and ordering the brilliantly coloured birds to fly away. The only people left to accompany him were his faithful servants, dwarfs and hunchbacks.

As he walked he came to a large tree where he stopped to rest and called for his mirror. Gazing at his reflection he saw that he had indeed become an old, tired man. In useless rage he flung stones at the tree trunk and they became so deeply embedded that they could be seen there for generations to come. In another place where he rested on a rock, the imprint of his hands and thighs were left as a permanent sign that he had passed that way. Whenever he was asked where he was going, he replied simply: 'I am going to learn.'

Still he walked and still his enemy Tezcatlipoca pursued him. Now in one form, now in another, he took from Quetzalcoatl all his skills: his knowledge of gold and silver working, of feathers, of leathercraft, of sculpture and painting. On the cold mountain slopes of the volcanoes Popocatepetl and Ixtaccihuatl, his remaining companions, the dwarfs and hunchbacks, died of cold and Quetzalcoatl was left entirely alone.

At last, alone and weary, Quetzalcoatl reached the sea. Using the last of his powers, he formed a raft of snakes and rode away on it across the sea.

Quetzalcoatl's story became an allegory of how a man must lose all the things of the earth if he is to learn about the spiritual world but it also had a special importance for the Spanish invaders of Mexico. The Aztecs believed that Quetzalcoatl would one day return from over the sea. This would happen in a year when his birthday fell on a particular day and one possible combination occurred in the year 1519. In the years before that, a series of omens seemed to foretell some important supernatural event and when the Aztec ruler, Montezuma, was told of the strange men who were landing on the neighbouring coast, he concluded that Quetzalcoatl had arrived to claim his land. Some traditions described Quetzalcoatl as a white man with a beard (unusual for an Aztec) and he was often shown in a pointed hat. The description of Cortez which the king's messengers brought seemed to identify him as the returning god and among the presents Montezuma sent to him were Quetzalcoatl's turquoise serpent mask, his feather ornaments and snake-shaped throwing stick.

It was only when the Spaniards revealed their warlike intentions that the Aztecs realized their tragic mistake.

The great journey

Before the Aztecs came to Mexico they lived far to the north of the Colorado river, in what is today the United States. Successive waves of migration brought the people gradually southwards and there are many legends which tell the story of the journey of the tribes. The different legends contain many conflicting details. Some are almost certainly historical records, passed on by word of mouth and naming people and places which can be identified by archaeologists. Others are more symbolic, explaining the moral or religious beliefs of the Aztec people.

In this story, the chief god of the Aztecs is Huitzilopochtli, whose name means literally Hummingbird of the Left or South. With

Quetzalcoatl the Feathered Serpent, Tezcatlipoca the Smoking Mirror and Xiutecutli the Yellow Fire, Huitzilopochtli was one of the great gods, a son of the original creators of the universe. When Huitzilopochtli was born he was at first only a skeleton, with neither flesh nor features. Later he was born again as a fully-grown warrior, God of the Sun and of War.

It is said that long ago the seven tribes of the Aztecs lived in Aztlan, the white land, in the place of seven caves. It was a land of plenty, with fish and waterbirds of all kinds, birds with brilliantly coloured feathers, meadows of grass and flowers, gardens of maize, chilli, tomatoes and beans. One day a man who was walking among the trees heard a bird calling urgently:
'Tihui . . . Tihui . . . Tihui . . .'

He stopped to listen and realized that the bird was calling out in the Aztec tongue the words 'Let's go, let's go, let's go.'
'What can it mean?' he asked his people, and since no-one could be sure, they went together to their chief Tecpaltzin.
'The bird is wise,' said Tecpaltzin when he heard their story. 'We have enemies in this place and it is time we found another land. I have known that this time would come and I have waited for a sign. This bird speaks for the gods.'

So the Aztecs gathered together and made an image of their great God, the Sun God, Huitzilopochtli. They placed the image on a bier of rushes and, holding him high at the head of their column, moved southwards to wherever he would lead them. Before they set out, Huitzilopochtli spoke to the priests: 'The place you seek is on the shores of a lake, far from here. There you will find an eagle perched on a cactus which grows from a wave-washed rock. In the eagle's talons is a great serpent, and the bird's spread wings glisten in the rays of the rising sun. Where you see this sign you must found your city.'

There were seven sub-tribes travelling together and they formed a great caravan of Indians, men, women and children, carrying all their belongings in bundles, leading their animals. The land they entered was very different from Aztlan. The ground was hard and stony and their feet were constantly cut by sharp thorns and thistles.

Snakes and rats slithered and scuttled among the sparse grasses and larger animals threatened to snatch the weaker members of the column.

On the long journey, the god Huitzilopochtli tested the seven tribes. He called the chief Tecpaltzin and said: 'Tomorrow morning there will be two bundles on the ground by the camp. One contains a bundle of sticks, the other a precious jewel. Let them choose which bundle they should take and I will judge who is the wisest.'

In the morning the two bundles lay where the god had said they would be and the tribes began to quarrel over them. At first everyone wanted to take the bundle with the jewel in it but then some of the more thoughtful people changed their minds. The jewel might be beautiful, but with sticks they could make fire, they could build shelters and make staffs and arrows. These would certainly be more use to them on their journey than a stone, however precious. So the tribes divided: the ancestors of the Aztecs chose the sticks while others chose the jewel and went their own way.

After many years of wandering and hardship, the Aztec tribes reached the city of Tollan and there they settled for a time, living in peace and prosperity. Some thought that this was their final home but the priests of Huitzilopochtli knew that they must go on. Many were reluctant; they had settled in Tollan, their children had been born there and knew nowhere else. Then Huitzilopochtli himself spoke to them: 'Do as I say and follow where I lead: I shall take on the form of a white eagle. I am your God, I am the Sun that looks after your lives, that warms and keeps you. Anyone who disobeys me and does not go my way is no true Aztec. Go only when you can see me and when I alight, you must stop. There you will see the sign, and there you will build my temple.'

The Aztecs listened respectfully and did everything that he commanded them. They followed him as he flew before them, a white eagle shining in the sunlight.

At last the Aztecs came to the Valley of Mexico and the swampy lake Tezuco. There among the reeds they found the sign they had been waiting for. A great eagle perched on a cactus that grew from a rock washed by the lake's waves. In its talons writhed a serpent and the eagle's wings were spread ready for flight.

Again the God spoke: 'From this place you will conquer all corners of the earth and subdue its peoples, for you are mine and there is no greater Sun God in all the world than I. Through strength and suffering you will gain everything you could desire.'

Archaeologists believe that the Aztec migration took altogether nearly three hundred years. The city which they founded in about 1320 was to become Tenochtitlan, the centre of the Aztec empire. When Cortez and his men entered it in 1519 they found a thriving city built on an island in the lake and approached by massive stone causeways. The land between the causeways had been built up using mud supported on wicker mats and formed floating gardens of vegetables and flowers. Aqueducts brought fresh water and the gardens and the city itself were criss-crossed by canals. Within the walls most of the houses were built of stone and were arranged around squares and paved walkways. In the great square a thriving market was filled with noisy throngs of traders from all over the empire.

Private dwellings were dominated by palaces of rose-coloured stone, temples to the gods and above all, by the vast temple pyramid to the War God Huitzilopochtli which rose to a height of over 356 metres in the centre of the city.

Tenochtitlan was totally destroyed by the Spanish conquerors in 1521 after a long blockade and fierce house-to-house fighting. Thousands of the Aztecs died from smallpox; starvation killed many who survived. It is said that in the final struggle Cortez and his men fought their way step by step to the platform top of Huitzilopochtli's temple, clearing it of four hundred Aztec warriors, then burning the shrines and destroying the images. Horrified by the evidence of human sacrifice which they had seen, the Spaniards razed the temples to the ground.

Today Mexico City stands near the site of Tenochtitlan. The Aztec symbol of the eagle and the serpent which led them on their long journey to their new home remains the national emblem of Mexico today.

The quarrel of the suns

They say that in the old days there were two Suns, one older and one younger than the other. One day Older Sun said to Younger Sun, 'Let's go and find some honey to eat.'
'I would love some honey,' said Younger Sun, 'but I have a sore leg. I won't be able to climb.'
'Never mind,' said Older Sun. 'I will climb.'
'And you'll give me some honey?'
'Of course,' said Older Sun. 'Why shouldn't I?'

The two Suns made their way into the forest and soon found a tree where there was honey. 'I'll climb up and throw you down some of the comb,' said Older Sun and he scrambled up the trunk and settled himself on a branch by the hole where the bees had built their nest. Soon he was gorging himself on the sweet liquid.
'Hey, what about me?' shouted Younger Sun.
'Just wait. I'll give you some in a minute,' said Older Sun thickly from the tree top. 'Here, open your mouth.'

Younger Sun stood looking up with his mouth open, and Older Sun threw down a large piece of comb. Unfortunately for Younger Sun, all the honey had already been sucked out of it, leaving only a mass of sticky wax.

Younger Sun protested loudly, but Older Sun claimed he was eating exactly the same thing. 'Here, try this piece,' he called, and threw down another lump of wax.

Younger Sun was angry. 'I'll give you wax,' he muttered to himself and he began to model little animals out of the beeswax and to place them in the ground around the base of the tree. One by one the little animals came to life until there was a crowd of agoutis rooting in the ground and gnawing at the tree roots. Older Sun, gorging himself on honey, noticed nothing until the tree began to sway and creak.
'What's happening?' asked Older Sun.

With a great creaking crash the tree fell full length on the forest floor. At that moment, Older Sun disappeared from the world, but in his place a herd of pigs appeared, the ancestors of all wild and domestic pigs today. It is said that their meat is rich and sweet because of all the honey Older Sun ate when he was in the tree.

The Mayas and their myths

The greatest of the ancient civilizations of Central America was undoubtedly that of the Mayas, who first arrived in the area around 2500 BC. They flourished in three regions to the south of the Valley of Mexico: in the highlands of what is now Guatemala from the coastal plain south of Chiapas in Mexico to the western half of El Salvador; in the lowland forests of northern Guatemala and Belize; and in the Yucatan peninsula. In early times they were influenced by the Olmec civilization of the Gulf of Mexico and it was from there that they took their calendar and writing systems. Their greatest period, however, was between AD 300 and 900. During this time they were at first influenced by Teotihuacan culture, from the great city eight hundred miles away in the Valley of Mexico.

When Teotihuacan collapsed around AD 600, the Mayas continued to develop in their own way. Great cities were built with stone buildings, many of which have now been reclaimed from the forest and restored to their former glory. Carvings, paintings and ornaments prove that the knowledge and skill of Maya craftsmen was far ahead of that of their contemporaries.

Towards the end of the tenth century, the Mayas came under the domination of the Toltecs, who brought with them a different style of art and architecture and new gods, including the Feathered Serpent god whom the Aztecs were to call Quetzalcoatl and the Mayas knew as Kukulkan. When the power of the Toltecs declined in the twelfth century, the Maya separated into independent kingdoms or states, the strongest of which were those of the Cakchiquels and the Quiché. By the time the Spaniards arrived, the greatest era of Maya civilization was already past. They were not, however, the first people to be conquered. The empires of central Mexico, with their riches of gold and precious stones, were higher on the invaders' list of priorities. Maya resistance took the form of a type of guerilla warfare and the Spanish were not able to establish a base in Yucatan until 1542. Missionary efforts were also later and less successful than among the Aztecs and indigenous religion and beliefs are far stronger in the area of the Mayas than elsewhere in Central America. Over forty Maya languages are still spoken and it is still possible to see Indians with the high sloping forehead and strong features that are so characteristic of ancient Maya portraits which have been preserved.

Much of what we know about Maya beliefs is taken from three sources, written down after the Conquest by experts from different Maya tribes. The *Chilam Balams*, from Yucatan, are a series of books which include songs, prophecies, historical events and details of ceremonies that were performed. The *Annals of the Cakchiquels* tell the legendary history of the Cakchiquels; and the *Popul Vuh* is a Quiché collection of legend and mythology which dates from the middle of the sixteenth century but was not discovered and translated until 1701.

The Maya did in fact have an elaborate system of writing and no less than twenty pre-Spanish codices or pictorial manuscripts have been found. Unlike the Aztec codices, however, any translations of these which may have been made at the time of the Conquest were lost or destroyed as works of the devil and efforts at deciphering the writing in later times have still not been entirely successful. It is likely that they deal with astronomy, ritual and ceremony rather than with legend and mythology but inscriptions on stone monuments suggest that actual history was also recorded.

Although Maya writing has not been fully deciphered, their mathematical and calendar system is understood. Like the Aztecs they used a system of mathematics based on twenties and with this were able to make very advanced astronomical calculations. Their calendar involved two separate cycles, one of 260 days and one of 365. Each day had its own omens and associations and each cycle of twenty days acted as a kind of fortune-telling device which guided the destinies of both individuals and state affairs. Using their calendar, it is possible to date the events they recorded with great accuracy.

The ball game *tlachtli*, which features in the story 'The twin brothers' on page 37, was played by the Mayas as by other Central American people. Some games seem to have been played for very high stakes, with the consequences of defeat being loss of liberty or of life itself. Near the remains of the ball court at Toltec Chichen in Yucatan, there is a long platform carved on all sides with human skulls impaled on stakes. This may give a grim idea of what happened to the losers of ritual games.

The gods dominated the lives of the Maya people but few stories are known about them and many do not now even have names. Scholars who have studied the pictures of the gods in the codices call them simply by letters of the alphabet: God A, shown with a skull's head, is probably the God of death, known in Yucatan as Yum Kimil; God G is a sun god, God I a water goddess and so on. The supreme god seems to have been called Itzamna, his consort Ix Chel and we know that the Feathered Serpent was Kukulkan. Other gods shown in the codices include a sky or star god, a maize god, a war god and a god of travellers and commerce. Gods of the elements and numerous animal gods are also known to have been honoured.

Unlike the Aztec gods, Maya gods and spirits seem on the whole to have been friendly towards humans and although sacrifice and blood penance were not unknown, they were not practised on a large scale. After death, the souls of humans journeyed to the kingdom of the dead but, as with the Aztecs, warriors and other special categories went to a kind of paradise, this time dominated by a large kapok tree which provided shade and gave eternal rest.

Spanish missionaries were particularly struck with what they considered to be similarities between Maya religion and Christianity. Both shared the story of the flood and had a ceremony of baptism and rebirth. Both used confession and penances and made pilgrimages to holy places. The Maya even knew the cross as a holy symbol, but to them it seems to have represented the four compass points. The similarities were so striking that some Spaniards even suggested that the apostle St Thomas had visited the land hundreds of years before on one of his missionary journeys.

Much exciting work remains for researchers to do into the ancient Maya world and it seems certain that new discoveries will be made which will increase our understanding of their way of life.

For their descendants in Central America, the spirit world is very much alive; though now influenced by many different cultures and traditions, the world of myth and fable is never far away from everyday life.

The first people

The *Popul Vuh* or Sacred Book of Advice, is a long and complex record of the myths of the Maya people. It was written down in the seventeenth century by a member of the Quiché tribe, a southern Maya tribe from the mountains of what is now Guatemala. Its name means literally 'The Collection of Written Leaves' and it contains a mixture of mythology, ancient legends and real history. Until recently, scholars were unable to decipher the Maya system of writing and the *Popul Vuh* provided our main source of information about the beliefs of the ancient Maya people. The sections here come from the first and third parts of the four-part book and deal with the creation of the world and with the migration and final settlement of the ancestors of the Quiché.

There was a time when everything was calm and silent and immobile, when the whole sky was empty. There were no people and no animals, no birds, fish, crabs, trees, stones, caves, gorges, grass nor woods—just the great sky and the sea, alone and tranquil. There was no earth, nothing that moved or made a noise; nothing stood out to break the calm horizon between sky and sea.

Above the surface of the sea it was always night but down below in the waters, surrounded by light, lived Pepeu and Gucumaz, the Creator and the Giver of Form. As gods, it was their nature to think about the mysteries of life and as they lay there, hidden beneath a canopy of green and blue feathers, they talked about the Heart of the Sky, the great god who had three parts, Cuculhá Huracán (the Lightning), Chipi Caculhá (the Streak of Lightning) and Raxa Caculhá (the Thunderbolt). As their thoughts ranged more widely they talked about life and brightness and decided that they would turn the darkness of night into day so that the world above would know light.
'Let there be brightness,' they said, 'a day that dawns over the sea and over a land which we shall make. And man shall be the first glory of the land.'

Everything happened as they commanded it. The seas shrunk into their new limits and the mountains appeared above the water to form dry land. With the mountains came the cypress trees and the pines while rivers rushed down among the rocks to the plains below. Everything was made by the Creator and the Giver of Form, helped by the three gods who were the Heart of the Sky.

When the mountains and trees were established, the gods made the small animals of the woods, the guardians of the forests and the spirits of the mountain: the deer, the jaguars and hyenas, the birds and the serpents. The Creator and the Giver of Form told each animal where to live—the deer by the side of the rivers, the cats among the forest undergrowth, the birds in the trees, the serpents in holes on the rocky hillsides. 'Speak our names, now,' said the Creator and the Giver of Form and the three gods of the Heart of the Sky. 'Our glory is not complete unless there is someone who can worship us.'

The animals could not do it: all they could do was cry or roar or cheep, each one making a noise according to its own nature.
'That's no use,' said the gods. 'These animals cannot even pronounce our names, let alone worship us.' Accordingly, the gods decreed that the animals they had made should be inferior and should be hunted and killed for food. Then the gods decided to create man.
'We must hurry,' they said, 'for dawn is coming and we need someone who will worship us.'

First, the gods made man out of mud from the bottom of the sea but they found this was unsatisfactory: the body was too soft and shapeless, his head flopped to one side, he could not turn his neck to look backwards and he had no strength in his arms and legs. He spoke but with no understanding and when they put him in the water, his muddy form dissolved and was lost in the swirling currents.

The Creator and the Giver of Form saw that this mud man would not suit their purpose and they held a consultation with the other gods, calling to their aid the Grandmother of the Day and the Grandmother of the Dawn, two ancient goddesses who could read into the future of all things. Together they formed men and women out of wood. These people looked like the mud man but unlike him they were strong and vigorous. Before long they produced children together and spread out over the land. Still they

had no understanding and they did not remember the Creator nor the Giver of Form. They shambled along clumsily, their eyes on the ground.

Finding that the creatures they had made were still useless to them, the gods destroyed many of them by sending a great flood to drown them and four giant birds to attack them. Even the animals among whom they lived came to harass them, accusing the people of treating them badly. Their kitchen pots and pans blamed them for not treating them with more respect: 'Night and day you have ground our surfaces with sticks and stones and burned us carelessly on the flames. Now it is your turn to suffer.'

Even the stones of the fireplaces threw themselves against the wooden men and hurt their heads. Many were destroyed in their houses, many others tried to escape, but it seemed that the whole world had turned against them. When they tried to clamber onto the roofs to escape, the houses collapsed under them; trees drew away as they approached; caves closed their open doors with giant boulders so that there was no place to hide. A few managed to reach the shelter of the forest and their descendants became monkeys, animals who chatter incessantly and make no sense.

Then the gods consulted together once more and before the first dawn broke they created the first human beings, making their flesh from white and yellow maize and their arms and legs from maize dough. With a special broth they gave the bones and muscles strength and power. The people they made first were men, named Balam-Quizé, Balam-Acab, Manucutah and Iqui-Balam. These four men were wise and good and could see things that are hidden from people today. The gods tested them.

'Look,' they said to the four humans, 'is not the earth a beautiful place? Look at the mountains and the valleys. Are they not good? Is it not good to be alive, to understand, to speak, and to move freely about?'

The four men looked at the world around them and agreed that it was a wonderful place. 'You gave us movement and sense,' they said. 'We speak and understand, we think and we move. From this one spot we can see everything, far and near, as clearly as we see each other. Praise to the Creator, praise to the Giver of Form.'

For a time the gods were satisfied with their humans but then they became worried in case the four men should become too wise. To prevent this from happening, the Heart of the Sky breathed cloud over their eyes so that they could no longer see clearly but saw the world as if they were looking through a misted glass. With their clear vision, the gods took away their wisdom and their perception of secret things, leaving them with only a distant sense of the mysteries of life. Otherwise, they felt, the four men, too, would become gods.

Although the gods took away wisdom, they gave the humans another gift, the gift of sleep. While the four men were sleeping, four beautiful women were brought to them to be their wives and in time the humans spread over the land. They lived peacefully together; everyone spoke the same language and prayed to the same gods, to the Creator and the Giver of Form, to the Heart of the Sky and to the Heart of the Earth. They prayed for children and for light—for the sun had not yet risen and the earth remained dark and damp from floods, and these humans had no knowledge of fire.

After a long time had passed and still there was no Sun to give light and warmth, the four brothers set out for Talan-Zuiva, the place of Seven Caves and Seven Valleys. Here they received the gods who were to be sacred to each family, one god for each clan. Balam-Quizé's clan god was named Tohil and his first gift to his worshippers was fire.

The brothers carried the flame carefully with them and when the rains came and extinguished it, Tohil struck a new spark from his shoes. News of the fire spread quickly and soon men from other tribes came to warm themselves and to carry a burning flame home with them. Tohil received them cruelly, demanding human sacrifices as the price of fire.

Still the Sun did not appear and the brothers fasted and watched for the Morning Star which they knew would be a sign of the first sunrise. At last, in despair, they decided that they would never see the Sun from the country where they were and they journeyed on through many lands until at last they came to the mountain of Hacavitz. As they burned incense at its rocky foot, they saw the Morning Star rise slowly over the shoulder of the mountain. Gradually the sky grew lighter and lighter until the great round disc of the Sun itself appeared.

The new Sun did not burn with the heat of the Sun we know today, but it was hot enough to dry

out the dank earth and make it more comfortable to live in. Before it appeared, great animals had roamed the land—giant tigers and jaguars, monster pythons and vipers. Now these, with the old clan gods, were turned to stone, their arms cramped like the branches of trees. The world was made a safer place for humans and the ancestors of the Quiché had found their mountain home.

The man of gold

Another creation story told by the Maya was collected in our own century. It tells how very long ago there were four gods. The earth had been created, the land was full of plants and animals and the sea was full of fish. The wind watched over everything, bringing different kinds of weather in due time. One thing was missing: there were no people.

'Let's make someone who will be grateful to us for all our hard work,' said one of the gods.

The others agreed and they began to discuss the best material to use. First they tried using mud. They modelled a little clay man and drew on it a face and features. When it was dry it looked very finely made but when they tested it in water its features dissolved and the whole body crumbled away.

Then they took a branch of wood and worked it with their knives, making limbs with fingers and toes, carving a delicate nose and mouth and hollowing out the eyes and ears. Pleased with the result, they tested it in water and it floated easily. 'We ought to see if he survives the test of fire,' said the first god, so they put the wooden man in the fire. The wood was dry and burned quickly; soon there was only a heap of ashes where the wooden man had been.

'Let's try gold,' said the third god, taking a large nugget out of his pocket. Once more the gods made a model of a man. They tested him in water and he did not melt; they burned him in the fire and he came out looking even better than before. 'He will do,' said the gods. 'Now he can praise us,' and they whispered words of thanks into the gold man's ear. But the gold man did nothing; he said nothing; he stared at them without seeing. Then the fourth god, who had been silent up to now, spoke. He was a very humble god, dressed not in splendidly coloured robes like the others, but in drab grey.

'Let's try flesh,' he said and before they could even reply, he had taken out his knife and cut off the fingers of his left hand. The fingers scuttled off on their own as fast as they could go, and became the first people. They were never tested in water or in fire—they ran off much too quickly for that—but soon there were thousands of them, scurrying around on the earth, finding out what was good to eat, which leaves protected them from the rain and which animals would and would not attack them.

The gods tried to keep an eye on them but the men moved so fast and looked so far away that the old gods could not follow their movements. The gods stretched and yawned sleepily and one by one they fell asleep, exhausted with the effort of creation.

One day the finger men discovered the man of gold. They approached him cautiously, waiting for him to speak or move, or smile. They offered him food to eat and water to drink, but he left them untouched. Growing bolder, the finger men touched him with their hands, but he felt cold and dead and made them shiver. However, he seemed important to them and when they travelled on, they carried him with them, looking after him as if he were alive. Slowly the gold man grew warmer until one day he became so warm that he spoke the words of gratitude that the four gods had planted in him.

As soon as they heard the word of thanks, the four gods woke with a start and looked around them. They saw all that the finger men had done and they were pleased with it, and they were pleased also with the words of the man of gold. 'The man of gold has turned out well, and the finger men, too, have done many things,' they said. 'The man of gold and his descendants shall be rich, while the finger men shall be poor. But let the rich men care for the poor men, since the poor men help the rich in their own way. And the poor men must answer for the men of gold before the Face of Truth. Our law is this: No rich man can enter heaven unless he is taken there by the hand of a poor man.'

The twin brothers

The ball game *tlachtli* was played in many parts of Central America in ancient times and the remains of several stone courts have been found. The rules are not known, but its aim seems to have been to strike a ball through a small hole in a circular stone. It was considered a noble and honourable game and there may have been inter-state or city matches with the players claiming clothes and jewels from the spectators as their reward. It is thought that the game also had a grimmer, ritual significance. In this story, it is at the centre of a struggle between the Lords of the Underworld and the twin heroes of the *Popul Vuh*.

There were once twin brothers named Hunhun-Ahpu and Vukub-Ahpu whose great passion in life was playing tlachtli. They spent all their time practising its skills and considered themselves the best players in the world.

It happened that the Lords of the Underworld, Hun-Camé and Vukub-Camé were also skilled players and, hearing the human brothers boasting about their prowess, they decided to challenge them to a game. Four owls were sent to the upper world as messengers and Hunhun-Ahpu and Vukub-Ahpu accepted confidently.

As they made their way to the Underworld kingdom of Xibalba the twins came first to a deep gorge, then to a river of boiling water and a river of blood. Finally they came to a place where four paths crossed. The paths were of different colours, one red, one white, one yellow and one black and as they stood wondering which one to take, a voice from the black path spoke to them. 'I am the way to the Lords of the Underworld. Take me.' Warily, the brothers proceeded.

Although the Lords of the Underworld were skilled tlachtli players, they suspected that the twins were even better and they decided to trap the brothers before they could prove their superiority. The twins were therefore not led straight to the ball court but were sent first of all to a great chamber where wooden images were seated among the real Lords of the Underworld. The images looked so lifelike that the twins bowed down to them politely and started their speeches of greeting. They had hardly spoken two words, however, when the sound of loud mocking laughter revealed their mistake. Furious that they had been ridiculed, the twins angrily challenged the Lords to fight. Once more the people of the Underworld deceived them. Pretending to usher the twins courteously to another chamber, they invited them to sit on two ornately carved stones. The twins accepted, only to find that the seats of the thrones were red hot. To the sound of more mocking laughter, they leaped into the air, howling with pain and rage.

Next the twins were taken to a vast underground cavern, the House of Gloom. Handing each one a torch, the Lords said: 'Guard these torches well and keep them burning brightly until the morning. If you fail, your lives will be forfeit.'

The torches, made of thin bundles of reeds,

soon burned away and the twins were left in the darkness to await their fate. When morning came at last they were led before the Lords of the Underworld.

'Where are your lights?' demanded the Lords.

'They are consumed,' replied the twins.

'Then you must die.'

The twins were duly sacrificed and their bodies were buried; the head of one, Hunhun-Ahpu, was hung in a tree as a trophy. This tree had never borne fruit before but no sooner had the head been hung there than a heavy crop of gourd-like fruits appeared, so that the head was hidden among them.

The Lords of the Underworld set the tree aside as sacred and forbade anyone to visit it but one day a young girl named Xquiq, overcome with curiosity, made her way to the tree and gazed up at its curious fruit.

'Will I really die if I touch one?' she asked, and she stretched out her hand to pluck one of them. From its place in the leaves, Hunhun-Ahpu's head looked at her and, as she held out her open hand, it spat into her palm.

'Hurry away to the upper world,' he told her, 'for through this spittle you carry within you my future sons.'

Astonished and frightened, Xquiq fled from Xibalba. Though the Lords of the Underworld tried to destroy her, she outwitted them, making friends with the owl messengers who pursued her and finally finding refuge with the mother of the dead twins. In due course she, too, became the mother of twins.

The new twins, named Hunahpu and Xbalanque, grew into strong young men, skilled hunters and quick-witted talkers. For as long as possible, their mother hid from them all signs of the game of tlachtli but eventually they discovered where their father's gloves, rings and rubber balls were hidden. Immediately they, too, became obsessed with the game at which they, like their father, excelled. Soon the sound of their practising reached the ears of the Lords of the Underworld.

'Who is that up there, shaking the earth with our game?' they demanded. 'Who dares to challenge us now? Come and play against us if you dare?'

Hunahpu and Xbalanque accepted the challenge just as their father had done and they, too, crossed the dangerous gorge and the rivers of boiling water and blood. When they came to the place where the four paths crossed they took the black one as they were directed. They, however, had come well prepared for the tricks of the Lord of the Underworld. They had brought with them an animal called Xan and when they entered the chamber where the wooden images were sitting among the Lords, they sent him ahead with instructions to prick the legs of everyone they could see. The first two figures were made of wood and made no sound when Xan attacked them, but the third cried out in pain and the twins greeted him politely. The animal picked out all the real Lords in the same way. The twins had passed the first test.

Next they were shown to the chamber with the red-hot thrones and here they simply bowed and turned back saying, 'These thrones are too good for us, we will sit on the ground.'

At the door of the House of Gloom, the twins were handed torches to light the way, but instead of using them they sat through the night in darkness, only lighting them when they heard the guards approaching in the morning.

At last the Lords of the Underworld agreed to play tlachtli with them, and, to their fury, were badly beaten.

The twins had won, but they were still in the kingdom of the Underworld and the Lords were not willing to let them escape easily. Seizing them roughly, they subjected the twins to a series of new trials. First they sentenced them to a night in the House of Cold, where glittering sheets of ice encrusted the walls and floor. The twins managed to keep warm by burning pine cones. Next came the House of Jaguars, where fierce animals howled for their blood. The floor was littered with the bones of former victims and the twins escaped by throwing these at the jaguars to distract their attention. They miraculously escaped burning in the House of Fire but in the House of Bats Hunahpu was nearly defeated. The twins had lain flat on their faces all night so as not to disturb the vicious bats which hung from the roof, but as day came, Hunahpu cautiously raised his head and was viciously attacked. With the help of a magic turtle who lived in the cave, the terrible wound was healed and the twins emerged from the ordeal stronger than ever.

Knowing now that the Lords of the Underworld could not overcome them, the twins decided to demonstrate their own powers. Pretending that they had been totally defeated, they allowed themselves to be burned on a great funeral pyre, round which all the Lords of the Underworld gathered to celebrate what they thought was a great victory. Their ashes were then scattered on the waters of an Underworld lake and there, thought the Lords, was the end of the boastful pair.

Five days later two strange creatures, half men, half fish appeared on the lake shore and the next day two decrepit beggars were seen in the Underworld. Ragged and useless as they seemed, they soon attracted attention by performing all kinds of magic tricks. They burned down houses and made them reappear as good as new, they made animals disappear and return, they even burned themselves and emerged a moment later completely unharmed.

The Lords of the Underworld were amazed. Having tested the beggars by allowing them to burn down the royal palace and the royal dogs (and bring them back as good as new) they commanded the beggars to burn them too. 'Can you, the Lords of Death, die?' replied the beggars. 'But if it will amuse you . . .'

With great ceremony they built a funeral pyre for the Lords of the Underworld and watched silently as they disappeared into the flames.

The people of the Underworld crowded round to see their Lords reappear but this time no miracle happened. Throwing off their disguise, the beggars revealed themselves as the twins and angrily explained that they had come to avenge their father.

'This is your punishment,' they declared. 'Because of your treachery, you are no longer worthy to play the game of tlachtli, nor to rule over men as you have before. Instead you shall be mere servants, grinding maize and making pots and pans. You shall have power only over the animals. Your power over men is defeated forever.' Then, after performing the funeral rites for their dead father and his twin, Hunahpuh and Xbalaque returned to the upper world.

Sipac and the maize spirits

The Achi Indians of Guatemala tell many stories about a giant named Sipac. Sipac was so large and so hungry that he would eat anything he could find—sometimes he even ate people. One day he was so hungry that he decided to sell some of his land to pay for food. In exchange for volcanoes, people from the coast offered him giant-sized loaves and he sold first one fiery mountain, then another in order to eat.

He wandered far and wide collecting his volcanoes and came one day to a place called Belejuj where there was a particularly fine one. He lifted it out of the ground easily and heaved it up onto his shoulders, hearing the water in its crater lake swishing around inside it. He was just setting out for the coast again to sell it when he saw three beautiful girls washing their hair in the river which had appeared in place of the volcano. The girls looked very similar except that their skin colour was different: one had white skin, one dark and the third red. All had long silky hair which hung down their backs. Although Sipac did not realize it, the three girls were three maize spirits, guardians of the earth, and their different colours represented three different types of maize. It was in their power to produce good harvests or to wither the cobs in the fields and so bring famine to the land. But Sipac simply saw three lovely girls.
'I'd like to marry you all,' he told them. 'Will you be my wives?'
'We would certainly like to have a strong man like you to look after us—and we have heard a lot about you,' said the maize spirits. 'We'll marry you on one condition: that you get us all our food from the river. Fish, crabs, frogs—these are what we eat. Do you agree?'
'Of course,' said Sipac, thinking it sounded very easy.

The three maize spirits had, however, decided to make fun of him. 'I can see that you are hungry,' said the youngest maize spirit. 'If you dive down under that stone you will find a big fat crab. You can eat that.'

She pointed to a great slab of rock deep down in the river bed and Sipac, eager to show off his strength, dived down and disappeared. He was down there for a long time, fumbling around trying to find the crab. Meanwhile the youngest maize spirit took off her head-band and cleverly twisted it into the shape of a crab. This she carefully hid under another rock in the water.

'Have you found the crab yet?' she called out to Sipac.

'No, I can't get it,' bubbled Sipac from under the water.

'Well, I've found another one here,' said the youngest maize spirit. 'Come up and try for this one instead.'

Sipac came to the surface, gasping for air and wondering if he had done the right thing in asking the three girls to marry him.

'Now I know there is a crab under that slab,' said the youngest maize goddess brightly, 'but the river is very deep there and the hole under the rock is more like an underground cavern than anything. I'm going to tie a chain to your legs so that we can pull you out if you get into trouble.'

Sipac did not like the idea of wearing chains but he was still enchanted by the beautiful girls and he submitted silently. The maize spirits held one end of the chain as he strode into the water and burrowed under the rock. When he was right out of sight underneath it, searching for the crab, the three maize spirits saw their chance. They jumped onto the rock themselves and began to wind the chain round and round it until it was securely fixed and Sipac was trapped.

At that moment Sipac found the crab made from the head-band and, realizing that he had been tricked, he tried to escape from under the rock. The chain held fast, but the maize spirits had not realized just how strong Sipac was. With the rock chained to his back, he staggered to his feet and ran off with great strides, too ashamed to look the beautiful maize spirits in the face again. In his haste he failed to look where he was going and when he came to a great gorge he fell right over the edge. He fell with such force that his giant body bored deep into the ground and the great stone he was carrying lodged fast on top of him and became a new volcano.

The volcano named Sipac is still there today, near the river Cala in Guatemala. Nearby is an enchanted village known as Pueblo Viejo, the Old Village, and if you go there you can often hear a deep rumbling noise from far down in the earth. That is Sipac rattling his chains as he sits under his rock, brooding about the three maize spirits who tricked him, the spirits of the white, the black and the red maize plants.

The spirit of the maize

In the days when people lived in peace and prosperity, the gods met together to discuss the situation.

'Man has become too comfortable,' they said. 'He has everything he needs to eat—he has meat, he has fruit, and, above all, he has maize. He doesn't seem to need us any more. He never makes sacrifices to us; we hear neither prayers nor praises. We might as well not be here at all.'

'I have an idea,' said one god. 'Let's hide the spirit of the maize. If they cannot find it, they will go hungry and then they'll realize they need us after all.'

The other gods agreed and together they hid the spirit of maize inside a large rock. Because the spirit was hidden, the crop of maize failed all over the land. Soon the markets were empty and the poor people were reduced to hunting for wild seeds and berries. Many people went hungry. The birds, too, missed the grains and husks which they used to peck from around the gardens and they began to search everywhere for the spirit of maize.

At last they found the great rock where the gods had hidden the spirit of the maize and they began to circle round it, wheeling and swooping down at it to peck the spirit out. However, the rock was much too hard for their beaks and they could make no impression on it at all. After a time an ant came wandering by.

'I'm going to eat you,' said one of the birds. 'I'm hungry.'

'That would be a mistake,' said the ant, 'because I am in a position to do you a good turn. I can show you how to release the maize spirit.'

'What do you mean?' said the bird. 'You're just a tiny ant and we are birds with strong, hard beaks. If we can't break open the rock, how can you?'

And he started to sharpen his beak so that he could spear the ant with it.

'You shall have the maize tomorrow,' replied the ant coolly,' and it would be very silly of you to lose the chance of a new supply of maize just for the sake of a tiny morsel like me. Be patient!'

'Well,' reflected the bird, 'perhaps you *are* rather small. We'll wait and see what happens tomorrow; it's possible—just possible—we may not eat you after all.'

The next day the birds gathered again at the great rock and saw to their amazement that there was a great heap of maize by the side of it. The gods saw it too, and hurried to distribute the seeds before the birds could eat them all up.

'Plant these new seeds carefully and tend them well,' they told the humans. 'And remember above all to pay more attention to the gods in future. Whenever you eat maize, think of us and give us thanks. If you fail to make your sacrifices and give us your praise, the maize may vanish again—and next time, who knows whether it will return.'

Then they turned to the ant. 'And how did you get into the rock?'

'It was quite easy,' said the ant. 'We came to the rock by night and the moon lit up all kinds of holes and crevices that no-one could see in the strong sunlight. Then we brought out the maize grain by grain, as we do when we take food to our anthills. There are so many of us that it was quickly done.'

'We didn't tell you that you could do that,' said the gods angrily. 'We hid the maize there for a purpose and you made us change our plans. Because of that we shall punish you. So that you remember not to poke around again in things that don't concern you, we shall tie you all up with a tight thread around your middle and fasten you to your anthill so that you will never be able to wander away again.'

The gods did as they threatened, but the ants were too clever for them once more. They managed to gnaw through the thread that attached them to their home and scurried away into a million holes and crevices in the ground. They did not escape the anger of the gods altogether, though, for the tight thread remained around their waists—and is still there to this day. As for the humans, they were grateful to the tiny ants and have treated them with respect ever since; even birds think twice before eating them up.

Why rabbits have long ears

There was once a jaguar who had arranged to marry a jaguar princess. He was walking along one day when a rabbit hopped up to him and said, 'I want to marry that jaguar princess. I'm cleverer than you are.'

'Oh no, you're not,' said the jaguar, very upset. 'You are nothing but a silly rabbit while I am a very strong and splendid jaguar.'

'We'll see about that,' said the rabbit.

The jaguar started to trot off but the rabbit kept up with him, boasting about his cleverness all the time. After a while the jaguar began to be irritated. 'Talking is not everything,' he said crossly. 'We'll go to the princess and prove who is the stronger and who can make the better husband.'

'Excuse me,' said the rabbit, 'but do you mind if I ride on your shoulders since you are so strong? I'm a bit tired of walking.'

The jaguar was pleased to hear this; it seemed to prove that he had nothing to worry about. 'Yes, of course,' he said condescendingly. 'Jump up.
'Just so that I don't fall off, let me put this saddle on,' said the rabbit casually, producing a small saddle from his bundle. The jaguar sighed loudly but did not protest. After a while the rabbit started to grumble and clutch at the jaguar's fur. 'Oh dear,' he said, 'I keep slipping. Do you mind if I put a bridle and bit on you? Then I'll have some reins to hold on to.'

Secretly pleased at another sign of weakness, the jaguar consented. 'Someone as strong as I am would never use such things, but I suppose you need them,' he said. 'The princess will have no difficulty in seeing which of us is the more powerful.'

By the time the rabbit had also put on spurs and was digging his heels into the jaguar's side and shouting at the top of his voice, the jaguar was not quite so sure of himself. And there was nothing much that he could do about it. Every time he tried to shake the rabbit off, the bit jerked painfully in his mouth and the spurs jabbed fiercely into his sides. A sharp sting on his rump told him that the rabbit had also produced a whip from somewhere and was belabouring him with that, too.

Unwillingly, the jaguar was forced to run right up to where the princess was living and to stop obediently. The rabbit smartly jumped off the jaguar's back and swaggered up to the princess, flicking back the grass with his riding whip. The jaguar slunk moodily behind a tree.
'I can see you are a pretty astute fellow,' said the jaguar princess, 'much cleverer than that rather stupid jaguar who wants to marry me.'
'Will you marry me instead, then?' asked the rabbit carelessly.
'Yes, of course,' purred the jaguar princess. 'But, well there's one thing. You are a bit small you know. Compared with the jaguar, of course. He is so strong and he has splendid teeth. Whereas you can't compete in that way . . .'
'I see what you mean,' said the rabbit, 'and I appreciate your feeling doubtful about me. Let us go to the Creator God to see what he can do for me.'

They travelled for several days before they finally found the Creator God sitting on a high mountain. The Creator listened attentively as the rabbit explained that he wanted to become a bigger and better rabbit, more worthy of the jaguar princess. After a long silence, the Creator answered. 'If you want to become bigger and better, you must find me three large teeth,' he said slowly. 'One tooth of an iguana, one of a giant and one of a monkey.'

The rabbit began with the easiest part of the task and hurried to the monkey's house. Posing as

a travelling barber, he offered to give the monkey a shave. After he had finished, he left his razor behind, knowing that the monkey would try to use it himself. As he expected, the next day the monkey started to shave and it was not long before he had cut his neck badly. With blood spurting, he ran to the door of his hut. Just then the rabbit happened to pass by.

'Help, rabbit,' cried the monkey. 'Help, I'm dying.'

'I'll only help if you give me that loose tooth of yours,' said the rabbit cunningly.

In desperation the monkey agreed and so the rabbit obtained the first tooth he required.

'That leaves two,' thought the rabbit and he set out to look for a giant. Before long he came across two giants who were walking along arguing angrily. The rabbit hopped onto a bank beside the path and threw a handful of stones at one of them.

'Why are you throwing stones at me?' shouted one giant to the other.

'I'm not,' replied the second.

'Yes you are,' cried the first.

Just then the rabbit threw a handful of stones at the second giant.

'Hey, now you're throwing them at me,' said the second giant. With that the two began to fight and in a moment or two they had each hit out with such force that they knocked each other unconscious.

The rabbit crept quietly up to one of them and looked into his open mouth. As he had hoped, one of his teeth had been loosened in the fight and the rabbit quickly pulled it out and ran away.

The third tooth was easy to get. The rabbit soon found an iguana sunning himself on a rock and suggested they play a game of catch. The rabbit produced a ball and threw it to the iguana, who caught it in his mouth and threw it back. When they had been playing for a few minutes, the rabbit substituted a round stone for the ball and threw it as hard as he could into the iguana's mouth, knocking out one of his teeth. Before the iguana had time to realize what had happened, the rabbit had snatched the tooth and run off.

With the three teeth securely in his paw, the rabbit made his way back to the Creator God.

'Ah,' said the Creator God, 'so you have managed to find the teeth. Well done. As a reward, you shall have them for yourself so that you and all your kind will have large, strong teeth to eat with.'

'But it's not only big teeth I want,' protested the rabbit. 'I want to be a giant-sized rabbit all over.'

'Oh, I see,' said the Creator God, laughing a little, and he leaned forward and gave the rabbit's ears a strong pull. 'Will that do?'

The rabbit's ears were now long and floppy. He rubbed them proudly with his paws and bounded back to the jaguar princess.

'Well, what do you think?' he said. 'I'm still not the largest animal in the forest, but I've the most splendid teeth, which will gnaw anything—and my ears are quite extraordinary.'

The jaguar princess took one look at the little rabbit sitting so proudly in front of her and started to laugh. 'You do look splendid,' she giggled, 'and I know you are clever, but you really won't do as a husband. I am expected to have some dignity, after all, and people will simply die of laughing when they see you. I think I'd better choose the old jaguar after all.'

So the jaguar princess and the jaguar were married and lived happily together. As for the rabbit, he and his children and his children's children have had big teeth and long ears ever since.

The man who became the sun

One hot afternoon a man was walking in the forest when he decided to have a rest in the branches of a tall tree. He climbed up, settled himself among the leaves and fell fast asleep. While he was sleeping, night fell and a band of thieves made their evening camp around the foot of the tree. They lit a fire, roasted their meat, ate it and soon fell fast asleep as well.

Their loud, satisfied snores awoke the man in the branches above their heads and he climbed down to investigate. He warmed his hands at the glowing fire and cautiously tasted some of the meat that was left lying in the embers. Finding it was good, he ate another piece, then another, until he had finished it all.

Then he looked around to see what else he

could find and soon discovered a chest which the robbers had stolen. Opening it, he saw a heap of beautiful clothes, made of the finest cotton, woven, dyed and embroidered with glowing colours. The man tried on garment after garment, strutting and posing in the firelight, holding out his arms to admire the colours and rubbing the soft cloth against his face. All this time the robbers snored contentedly around the fire.

At the very bottom of the chest the man found a beautiful red cloak and he wrapped it lovingly around his shoulders. At once something strange began to happen: his feet began to move of their own accord, making delicate dancing steps he had never known before. Faster and faster he danced, becoming wilder and more uncontrolled, swooping and bending, shouting, now leaping in the air, now crouching to the ground before kicking out with both feet at once.

One of the thieves, disturbed by the noise, opened a sleepy eye and then closed it again quickly. 'What a horrible dream,' he thought. Then, 'Is it a dream? A man all shining in red, dancing like a madman by the fire?'

The thief opened just one eye so as not to have too much of a shock. There it was again. There really was a wild man dancing by the fire, dressed in a bright red cloak.

The thief let out a piercing scream, waking his companions with a start. 'It is the spirit of the mountains,' they whispered to one another. 'He has come to devour us!' In a panic they leaped up and rushed away into the forest.

The dancing man did not even notice them; he danced on and on, moving away from the fire, through the trees and on to the edge of a great precipice which seemed to separate the earth from the sky. Without hesitating for a moment, the man danced over the edge of the precipice, out into the darkness which had no end. Instead of disappearing into the void, however, the dancing figure seemed to hover for a moment in space, then, with his cloak whirling round his shoulders, he began to soar into the air. Higher and higher he rose until he no longer looked like a man in a red cloak, but like a bright red circle in the sky. Rising higher and higher, a glow of light began to spread from him and the air grew warm around him. The dancing man had become the sun.

The grapefruit girl

There was once a king who chose a girl for his son to marry. The girl was beautiful and intelligent but the son did not like her.
'I want to marry a wife who was not born in the usual way,' he said. 'I want a magic wife from the world of plants.'

Everyone thought this was very strange but the king was an understanding father and he did not insist on his choice. Instead he waited to see what kind of girl the prince would find for himself. One day the prince was walking along a path through the forest when he met a very old man. Although the prince did not know it, the old man was in fact the Creator God.
'Where are you going?' asked the Creator God.
'I'm going to look for a wife from the plant kingdom,' replied the prince. 'A woman straight from nature.'

The Creator God searched in his hunting bag and handed the prince three objects: a stone, a cup with some water in it and a thorn.
'Take these,' he said, 'and you will find what you want. But beware. There are bad people about who will try to prevent you from finding her and will try to harm you both.'

The Creator God disappeared into the forest and the prince continued to walk along the path, studying the plants that crowded on either side. Before long he came to a grapefruit tree with ripe fruits hanging on its branches. He was feeling hot and thirsty so he plucked one and cut it in half with his knife. 'Give me water,' he said, but the fruit was dry and hard inside and had no juice. He took another from the tree and cut it in half, but it was just the same. He reached up a third time and was holding the grapefruit in his hand ready to cut it when to his astonishment it turned into a woman.
'Ah, that's what I wanted,' said the prince, 'a woman from the natural world, not an ordinary human being like all the others.' Taking the woman gently by the hand he continued on his journey.

They had not travelled very far when they realized they were being followed by evil robbers. However fast they went and however many

twists and turns they made through the forest, they were quite unable to escape; the sound of footsteps and breaking twigs behind them simply grew louder. At last the prince remembered what the Creator God had said and he took the thorn the God had given him and threw it down on the path behind him. Looking back he saw that a great thicket of thorns had sprung up, completely blocking the way. He could hear the pursuers cursing as they struggled in the tangled branches. The prince and the grapefruit girl hurried on. Soon, however, they heard the sounds of footsteps once more and realized that the robbers had managed to break through the thorn barrier. This time the prince threw down the stone the God had given him and immediately a great mountain grew out of the ground behind them, jagged with rocks and ravines. The sounds of pursuit died away and the prince and the grapefruit girl walked on more slowly, certain that the robbers would not be able to climb the mountain and catch up with them. At night they slept among the grass and flowers under the shelter of a tall forest tree and in the morning they set out again hand in hand. To their alarm, they began to hear the familiar rustling noises again. 'Surely we must be imagining it,' said the prince. 'How could they have climbed the mountain so quickly?' They stopped to listen. There was no mistaking the sounds; the robbers were back. 'This is our last chance,' said the prince, and he took the cup of water he had carried carefully all this time and emptied it out on the ground behind them. As they watched, the water spread out further and further, engulfing the plants and trees, stretching as far as they could see, a mighty ocean with high white-capped breakers turning to calmer waves which lapped gently at their feet. The robbers were swallowed up in the deep water and the prince and the grapefruit girl were safe.

The mountain that had grown from the stone formed one boundary of the new ocean and now that the robbers had disappeared, the prince and the grapefruit girl decided to climb it so that they could see how far the ocean extended. They stood on the very top of the mountain, gazing round at the sparkling water which seemed to stretch forever. Far away they thought they could faintly see the familiar hills of the prince's own country. 'Look,' said the grapefruit girl suddenly. 'There's a well here. The water is so clear that I can see my face in it.' She leaned over, gazing at her reflection. The prince continued to stare into the distance.

At that moment a dark, rough-looking woman crept up. She saw the tall, strong prince and fell instantly in love with him. Then she, too, approached the well and saw the reflection of the grapefruit girl's face.

'Oh how beautiful I am,' said the dark woman, looking into the well, believing the face she saw in the water was her own.

'You may feel beautiful,' said the grapefruit girl sharply, 'but you certainly have an ugly face.'

Angrily, the dark woman took a long thorn from her skirt and pressed it into the grapefruit girl's arm, turning her into a small white dove which circled round a few times then flew away over the ocean. The prince, absorbed in planning his route home, saw and heard nothing and when

he turned round to explain it to the girl, at first he did not notice that she looked different. Then he seemed to doubt.

'But you've become very dark skinned,' he said. 'Are you sure you are the same grapefruit girl I took from the tree?'

'Yes, of course,' said the witch, muttering a quick spell to cloud his eyes. 'It's just that I've been out in the sun on this mountain for too long and you did not give me anything to protect my skin from the heat.'

'Well I suppose you must be my beloved grapefruit girl, since I can't see her anywhere. I'll take you to my father and tell him I want to marry you.'

After a long journey, the prince and the witch arrived back at the king's home.

'Here is a girl who came from a grapefruit, father,' explained the prince, 'and she is just what I wanted. Or more or less,' he added, still rather puzzled about the change in the girl.

'Hmm,' said the king. 'She's a bit ugly, isn't she?'

'Well, she got rather sunburned on the top of a mountain,' explained the prince. 'And she's tired from the journey.'

Just then a little dove flew over the royal palace and went fluttering around the garden, calling 'I want my prince, I want my prince.' Several of the gardeners working there heard it and in time the story reached the prince himself.

'Catch that dove and bring it to me,' he ordered and they brought him the little white bird in a wooden cage.

'I want my prince,' it cried sadly but although the prince questioned it again and again, it could say no more. The prince did not suspect, of course, that this was the real grapefruit girl and though he cared for the little dove and kept it always in his room, he did not understand what it was trying to tell him.

At around this time a war began between the king's people and a neighbouring tribe. Since the king was now rather old, the prince offered to lead the army in his place. As soon as the prince had left, the witch (who knew exactly who the little white dove really was) seized her chance to destroy her rival forever.

'I'm really feeling like a nice roast dove for my supper today,' she announced to the king. 'That one in the cage who is always making that wretched noise would do well.'

The king had no objections and ordered his servants to kill the dove. They were just about to kill it when, to their surprise, it cried out, 'Please don't cut me up. Bury me in the garden.'

The frightened cook secretly buried the little dove in the garden as it asked. He prepared another bird for the witch and she ate it greedily, thinking to herself that at last she was safe from the grapefruit girl.

When the little dove was buried in the ground it was in a sense returning to its natural element, for the grapefruit girl had originally come from the plant world. Down in the darkness it slowly put out roots and soon a slender green shoot appeared above the soil. With unusual speed it grew into a tall, beautiful grapefruit tree and when the prince came back from the war it was already hung with large, pale golden fruit. It happened that soon after the prince's return it was the king's birthday and the prince asked him what he would like to eat.

'I cannot think of anything I would like more than a grapefruit from that beautiful tree that has grown in the garden. I have always been grateful to you for taking my place and that tree somehow meant a lot to me while you were away.'

'Let me pick one for you,' said the prince, who also felt curiously attracted to the tree. As he reached up to pluck the fruit, memories of the day he had found the grapefruit girl came flooding back. Holding the fruit gently in his hand he whispered 'Give me water' as he had done before. There beside him once more stood his beautiful grapefruit girl, smiling with happiness at being restored to human form. The prince, too, was overjoyed. All the things that had puzzled him before—the strange dark woman, the little talking dove—became clear and he found it hard to understand how he could have been deceived for so long. Angrily, he ran to find the evil witch who had tried to destroy his wife, but there was no sign of her. As soon as she had seen the grapefruit girl returning unharmed, she had simply burned up with rage and was never seen there again. As for the prince and the grapefruit girl, they were married at last and lived together happily for the rest of their long lives.

The first domestic animals

There was once a young god whose older brothers were very unkind to him. The little god lived with his mother but his brothers had moved to a house nearby and he often went there to eat. It would be more accurate to say he went to watch them eat, for the truth of it was that they did not often give him anything worth while in the way of food, although they ate well themselves. In those days there were no domestic animals and since the little god was too young to hunt, he often went hungry.

One day they were all sitting round the table when he came in. The older brothers were eating meat.

'Sit down over there,' one of them ordered the little god, 'and see if you like these!' And they started to throw the bones of what they were eating to him, as if he were a dog. 'Go on, gnaw on those bones, there's a good child,' they said, roaring with laughter at their own cleverness.

The little god did not laugh but he gathered up the bones they pelted at him and put them in a sack, saying gravely, 'Thank you, brothers, you are very kind.'

When he got home he showed the bones to his mother. 'Do you know what I'm going to do?' he asked her. 'I'm going to plant these bones in the ground and see what grows.'

'My dear child, one of those bones must have hit you on the head and made you mad,' said his mother worriedly. 'Those are dead bones; they won't do anything in the ground but rot away. Don't be so silly!'

The little god was not put off and he planted the bones in orderly rows in the garden, starting with the biggest and ending with the smallest. His mother decided to let him do what he pleased, thinking that at least he would be amused for a while.

The little god went to inspect his garden every day and after three days he saw something beginning to show itself through the ground. Excitedly, he ran to his mother. 'Mother, the backs of the animals are coming up through the soil,' he said.

'Don't be silly, son,' she replied, laughing at him.

'The rain has just washed away the topsoil where you planted the bones, so that now you can see parts of the bones you planted there.'

She was wrong. Every day when the little god went to look at his garden, a bit more of the animals was visible and soon even the mother had to agree that something amazing was happening there. One morning the little god found a herd of cattle grazing where the largest bones had been planted. Once more he ran to the house. 'Mother, there are cows there now! And there are others coming out of the earth: sheep and goats and pigs. Come and see.'

One of the first things they did was to kill a fine young bull to celebrate their new wealth with a good meal of meat. When they had eaten every morsel, the mother decided to send some of the bones over to the older brothers' house to see what they would say; she thought they might well be rather angry. In fact the brothers were worried as well as angry.
'Where did he get such a huge beast from?' they asked one another. 'These bones have not come from any ordinary herd. Is he going to be richer than the rest of us?' Then they started to grumble. 'What does he mean by sending us bones from his feast? He's trying to patronize us.'

Finally they decided to go and see where their little brother was keeping his animals. 'If they are in a cattle pen or fenced in a field, we'll just scatter them. All we have to do is break down the fence.'

They found the animals' home with no trouble: they were grazing contentedly together in a large grassy area, surrounded by a high wooden fence. The oldest brother turned to the second. 'Turn yourself into a woodpecker, brother and make holes in the fence so that it falls down. Then the animals will run away—and who knows we might take some for ourselves.'

The second brother changed himself into a sharp-billed woodpecker and began pecking away at the fence as hard as he could. However, although he kept insisting that he was making progress, the fact was that the wood was very hard indeed and he was hardly marking the surface. In the end, with his beak quite badly bent, and the fence standing as firmly as ever, he gave up. The oldest brother had another idea. 'Let four of us turn into moles and burrow our way in. If we each

start at one corner . . .' This was slightly more successful than the first plan, for the moles managed to undermine the four corner posts with their tunnelling and some of the animals escaped and fled into the forest. Before they could all be scattered, however, the little god heard the sound of their hooves and came running to see what the matter was. The brothers, frightened to face their little brother now that he had become so mysteriously rich, ran off. The little god repaired the fence with wooden posts that were even stronger than the first ones.

The little god never found the animals who escaped and in the forest they became the wild animals that live there now. The cattle became wild buffalo, the pigs wild boars, the sheep and the goats, deer. Those that remained in the pen, more docile and obedient creatures than their runaway cousins, were the ancestors of our domestic animals.

The marriage of the sun and the moon

There was once a man who had a beautiful daughter. Every day she sat working at her loom and every day she saw a young hunter pass by her door on the way to the forest. In the evening he always returned with a deer slung across his shoulders.

One day she was washing some maize before cooking it and she threw the water onto the path in front of her father's hut. The maize water made the path very slippery and as the young man passed he fell down. The deer he was carrying fell from his shoulders and the girl saw that it was not, in fact, a freshly killed animal but a skin full of red hot ashes which scattered all around, smouldering and smoking. The young man was no ordinary hunter but the Sun himself. Now, ashamed to have been unmasked, he turned into a hummingbird and flew off as fast as he could.

The Sun man remembered the girl who had discovered his secret and returned the next day in his hummingbird form to feed on the flowers in her garden.
'Catch me that lovely bird,' she asked her father and he aimed his sling at the bird and brought it

down, stunned. The girl took the tiny bird gently in her hand and held it close to her all the day. At night, when her father locked her in the warmest and safest part of their hut, she took the bird with her.

In the warmth of the room, the hummingbird revived and saw the girl fast asleep by the fire. Taking on the shape of a young man again, he woke her up.

'Come, it is I. Let's escape,' he whispered.

The girl recognized the young hunter at once and was very pleased.

'I'd come with you but my father has locked the door and if we run away he will catch us and kill us.'

'No he won't,' replied the hunter, 'for I can change our shapes.'

'But he has a magic lens which will show him where we've gone to,' she protested.

'Don't worry,' said the young hunter. 'I'll take care of that.'

In a moment, the two had changed their shapes and escaped through the keyhole. Before long they were far away from the girl's home.

Next morning the father discovered that his daughter had disappeared and immediately guessed what had happened. 'That was no ordinary hummingbird,' he said. 'Whatever it was it has bewitched her.' Taking his magic lens, he held it to his eye so that he could see where they had gone to. It was no use. The young hunter had sprinkled the lens with hot chilli powder which made the father's eyes smart and water so much that he could barely see at all.

Rushing out of the hut he called to the volcano that towered over the village, 'Volcano, volcano, stop my runaway daughter and the young man with her. Stop them and destroy them!'

A rain of fire and sparks suddenly shot out of the volcano's summit, roaring towards the young couple as they ran along. Just as it reached them, the hunter saw a tortoise at the roadside.

'Let me into your shell,' he cried.

'How can I do that?' replied the tortoise grumpily. 'There's hardly room for me in here as it is.' But the young hunter was a shape-changer and, making himself very small indeed, he crept in beside the tortoise. He was just saying the words which would enable the girl to join him when the rain of fire engulfed her and she was scattered into a thousand fragments.

The rain of fire was followed by a flood and when the young man emerged at last from the shell, he saw that the girl was scattered over a great lake. He ordered everyone to collect the pieces and put them in water in hundreds of skins and pots and containers of all kinds. When they were all full, he put them in a bag and took them to an innkeeper, explaining that he would come in two weeks to reclaim it. After some days, the innkeeper was horrified to see the bag moving and when the young man returned he asked him what was in it.

'All is well,' said the young man, 'look.' When he opened the bag, all the bottles and skins and pots and containers were full of little animals and in one bottle, very small indeed, was the tiny figure of a girl. When she saw him she waved and smiled at him happily: the girl had been brought back to life.

All that remained to be done was to restore her to her normal size and this the young man achieved by his powerful magic. The young hunter resumed his duties as the Sun and when the girl became his wife soon after, she became his Moon.

The Incas, children of the Sun

At the end of the fifteenth century, the empire of the Incas was at its height, occupying nearly 35,000 square miles and stretching some 3,000 miles along the coast and mountains of western South America. The Incas traced their dynasty of emperors from AD 1200 but real historical information is available only from 1438, when the emperor (or Inca) Pachacutec came to power.

Before his time, the Inca people had probably been permanently settled around Cuzco in south-eastern Peru. Essentially a mountain race, the Incas were most at home in the high Andes country. There they became skilled in agriculture of all kinds, growing maize and potatoes, fruit, vegetables and cotton and using domestic animals such as the llama and alpaca for food, wool and as beasts of burden. Weaving and pottery were expertly done and they had good knowledge of medicine, including surgery. They had no writing but kept accounts and other records by means of *quipus*, a complicated system of coloured and knotted cords. Above all, perhaps, they were brilliant engineers and builders. Although they did not invent the wheel, and had no iron, they constructed massive buildings with a precision that would be impossible to match today. In Sacsahuaman, the fortress overlooking Cuzco, there are perfectly carved stones each weighing a hundred tons or more and fitted together so exactly that even a knife blade cannot be slipped between them. The city of Machu Picchu, which was rediscovered in 1911 and lies above the Urubamba valley, some seventy-five miles north of Cuzco, is one of the most impressive sights in the world. The Incas' engineering skills enabled them to develop sophisticated irrigation techniques and much of their military success was made possible because they were able to control the water supply of the fertile valleys they wished to conquer. Engineering knowledge was also put to good use in constructing terraces for growing food and there are places where terraces were shaped to take account of a mountain ridge far above, so that the plants received as much sun as possible.

The Inca Emperor Pachacutec was not only a great builder but also an aggressive and successful general and an astute ruler. He began the expansion of the Inca empire, which continued under his son Tupac Yupanqui, who succeeded him in 1473. Tupac conquered the Quito people of what is now northern Ecuador and on the coast overran the Chimu kingdom with its great city of Chan Chan and all the oasis valleys to the south, including the future site of Lima. He then pushed further south along the Pacific coast, taking the Nazca valley and establishing Inca rule as far as central Chile. He also conquered many highland areas of what is now Bolivia. The expansion was undertaken with almost religious fervour, with the Incas claiming they were bringing faith, knowledge and practical skills to help more ignorant peoples.

Roads and communications were good in the empire and relays of runners called *chasquis* carried messages from one end of the empire to the other. Armies could be moved easily and swiftly and rebellions were quickly suppressed. To make it even more difficult for conquered peoples to rebel, whole populations were moved from their own areas to different parts of the empire, so that if they did try to fight, they would be at a disadvantage in unfamiliar surroundings.

The empire was divided into four quarters, with the centre at Cuzco, the ancient Inca capital. At a local level, administration was based on clan groups and family relationships. The state was a blend of dictatorship and socialism: the common people were protected from hunger and real hardship but their actions were severely controlled. The class system was rigid and ordinary peasants and workers had to provide for a large class of nobles and priests.

Tupac's son Huayna Capac inherited his father's vast empire but it was by now too extended for one man to rule and there was soon conflict between the northern and southern halves. When the Spaniard Pizarro arrived in Peru with 180 men, two rulers were contesting the leadership. Atahualpa, based on the northern city of Quito, was fighting Huascar in the south, based on Cuzco. Atahualpa emerged the winner but was himself captured by Pizarro in 1533. As a ransom he offered to fill a room 8 metres by 5 metres with gold and Pizarro eagerly accepted. Llama loads of gold soon started to arrive, mostly from the Temple of the Sun at Cuzco. Pizarro duly signed a document agreeing that the ransom had been paid but he kept Atahualpa in captivity and later brought charges against him and had him executed.

The conquest by the Spaniards brought Inca civilization to a sad end. Once their religion had been overthrown and their way of life destroyed, many people seemed to lose all will to live. Mortality rose to sickening proportions, with tens of thousands dying. Those who survived had no choice but to provide cheap labour for the Spanish conquerors.

Why was it so easy for Pizarro, with no more than 180 men and a few horses, to conquer the great Inca empire? One possible reason comes from Inca mythology. Like the Aztecs, the Incas worshipped a fair-skinned god, who they said had sailed away to cross the Pacific from the western shores, saying that one day he would return. Pizarro, like Cortez before him, seemed to fit the description.

Inca religion joined together different beliefs from the tribes they conquered and early Spanish travellers who wrote down their impressions of the country and its people soon after the conquest, recorded many different versions. The supreme Inca god was Viracocha but he seems to have been more a god of the Inca elite than of the common people. The Sun god Inti, Mamaquilla, the Moon, Illapa, Thunder and, above all, Pachamama, the Earth Mother, were more popular deities and were worshipped with both elaborate rituals—as in the Temple of the Sun—or in simple village ceremonies. The Inca emperors claimed that they were directly descended from the Sun god himself.

Popular shrines were called *huacas* and could be natural objects such as caves, hills or springs or household objects made out of pottery. Anything in nature which looked unusual was regarded as sacred: oddly shaped stones, animals with some peculiarity, even twins, were all holy objects.

Today Inca beliefs and their language, Quechua, survive among some eight million people in the Andean mountains. As more and more people are lured from their traditional homelands to the expanding towns the pressure on them to abandon their culture and become 'westernized' becomes greater and greater. The great stone monuments which survive from their past are a lasting reminder of their achievements.

The first Incas

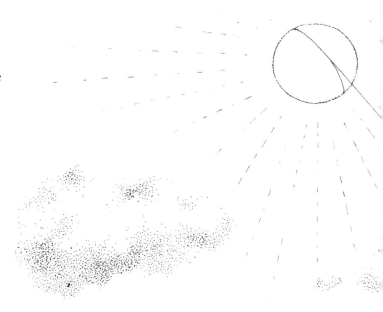

The Spanish chroniclers who first wrote down the myths and legends of the Inca people recorded many different versions of the creation of the world and of the coming of the Incas. In one, the great Creator God, Viracocha, decided to make a world for men to live in. First he made the earth and sky. Then he began to make people to live in it, carving great stone figures of giants which he brought to life. At first all went well but after a time the giants began to fight among themselves and refused to work. Viracocha decided that he must destroy them. Some he turned back into stone—and these can be seen today as the great stone statues of Tiahuanaco and Pucara; the rest he overwhelmed with a great flood. When the flood subsided it left behind the great lakes of Titicaca and Poopo and it is still possible to find sea-shells in the hills, left there when the sea roared up onto the Altiplano, 3,660 metres above sea level.

Viracocha saved two of the stone men from the flood and with their help he created a new race of people of his own size. The world was still dark and Viracocha could not see to admire the new men he had made, so he reached down to the bottom of Lake Titicaca and drew out the Sun and the Moon. Now the world was bright by day and even brighter by night, for in those days the Moon was even brighter than the Sun. It was only when the Sun grew jealous and threw a handful of ashes onto the Moon's face that they became as they are today.

Viracocha then decided to make a race of people who would be superior to all the humans he had created so far and in a place called Paqaritambo, where there are three small caves, he called forth a new race of men and women. From the two side caves came the ancestors of the Inca villagers but from the cave in the centre came four brothers and four sisters who were to be the founders of the Inca royal family.

Instructing them to found a mighty empire, Viracocha sent the brothers and sisters out into the world. They travelled slowly across the country, staying a year in this place, two years in that, learning about the world. Soon, one of the brothers, Ayar Kachi, whose name means 'salt' began to cause trouble. He was the strongest of the four and loved to play with great stones and rocks, throwing them at the hillsides and opening great ravines as he did so.

'Ayar Kachi is growing too strong,' said the brothers and sisters. 'He will destroy the country completely.' Pretending that there was a vast treasure hidden in a mountain cave, they tricked Ayar Kachi into entering it, then blocked the entrance securely and trapped him inside.

Next, the second brother, Ayar Ucho, whose name means 'pepper', decided to remain in the village of Huanacuari. 'Here I shall found a shrine and here, turned to stone, I shall remain. As its central idol I shall be immortal,' he said.

The third brother, Ayar Sauca, whose name means 'joy' chose to remain among the peasants, looking after the sowing and harvesting and being honoured as a spirit of the fields.

The fourth brother, Ayar Manco, and his four sisters came at last to the place where Cuzco stands today.

'Let's found our capital city here,' said one of the sisters, Mama Ocllo, and they struck the ground with a golden wand to determine exactly where the centre of the city should be. As they began to build, it became obvious that it would not be an easy task. There were no hills around the site they had chosen and it was quite without shelter. A

terrible wind blew day and night and even stones could not stand against it.

Ayar Manco decided the only thing to do was to catch the wind and keep it inside a llama pen until he had built the city, and this, with great difficulty, he managed to do. One day, however, the brother who had stayed behind in the fields heard the wind roaring as it tried to escape. 'What are you doing with my wind?' he demanded. 'You cannot imprison a free spirit like that.'
'What else can I do?' asked Ayar Manco. 'Every time I try to build a house or a temple, the wind blows it down again.'

Now Ayar Sauco loved the wind and looked on it as his own, for in his home the wind howled round him every day and he felt lost without it. However, he sympathized with his brother so he said, 'Very well, you may keep the wind in the llama pen for just one day but then you must let it go. In that day you must build Cuzco and the great Temple of the Sun.'

Ayar Manco was in despair. How could he finish building a great city and temple in just one day? Then he had an idea. Taking a strong rope he climbed a high peak in the mountains and threw a loop round the Sun as it passed overhead. He tied the end of the rope to a great rock, tethering the Sun in the sky so that it could not complete its daily journey. In this way he stretched the day into weeks and months; during all this time it

never grew dark and the Sun never set. Today the high rock above the City of Machu Picchu is known as 'The hitching post of the Sun'.

By the time he freed the Sun once more and the long, long day came to an end, the great city of Cuzco was built, and the Temple of the Sun stood in its centre. Now Ayar Manco opened the llama pen and the wind fled away to the mountains. To keep it away from the new city, Ayar Manco caused great mountains to rise up and surround it so that the wind could never again destroy the work of men's hands.

From that time forward Ayar Manco was known as Manco Capac, the Rich King and Lord and he and his wife and sister, Mama Ocllo, became the first Inca rulers.

A second legend tells how the Inca rulers were descended from the Sun itself. According to this, there was a time long ago when people had no houses and no cities. They did not know how to plough or to spin, they knew nothing about the gods and lived with no ambition or purpose in life except to eat and keep warm. Living in caves and dressed in skins, they lived on the very edge of human existence.

When the Sun looked down on the humans he pitied them for he knew they were capable of better things and he decided to send his son and daughter down to instruct them in the arts of civilization. Before the two left him, he gave them a golden rod half a metre long and the width of two fingers.
'Wherever you stop to eat or sleep, you must sink this rod into the ground. In most places the ground is hard and the rod will not go in. But one day you will come to a place where the rod sinks in as if into water and there you will build the city of Cuzco. It will be called the sacred city of the Sun, for my temple will be built there and all the people will know me.'

The Sun also explained how his children should look after the people they taught, how to care for them as the Sun cared for the earth, as a father for his children. Then he set the two down on the Island of the Sun, in the Great Lake Titicaca and they began their work in the world.

From Titicaca the two children of the Sun travelled northwards, and wherever they rested they always tried to push the golden rod into the earth. At last they came to a beautiful valley and there, at a place called Huanacauri, they slid the golden rod into the earth to its full height, as if it was sinking into water.

'This is where we shall build our father's temple,' said the Inca, the child of the Sun.

Then the Inca Manco Capac travelled northwards and his sister-wife Ocllo Huaco returned southwards again to gather together the peoples who would form the Inca nation. Everywhere they went they were recognized as the children of the Sun and given obedience and honour. People were eager to join them and to build houses and temples under their guidance. As the city started to grow, the children of the Sun taught the people how to break up the soil and cultivate it, how to sow crops of grain and grow vegetables and fruit. They taught them to make ploughs, to cut irrigation canals, to keep llamas for meat and wool and to make shoes from their skins. The sister-wife taught the women how to weave and make clothes and how to prepare and cook the new foods they ate.

In this way the children of the Sun, the first Inca rulers, brought peace and prosperity to the whole land as their father had intended.

The legend of the lake

Lake Titicaca, the largest freshwater lake in South America, lies nearly 4,000 metres up on the high plain known as the Altiplano, straddling the border between Bolivia and Peru. To the Incas, the lake was a holy place, for it was there that the children of the Sun first descended to earth. This story, set in a region where earthquakes are still a common occurrence, explains how the lake first came into being.

Long ago in the high plains lay a vast, rich city built by a proud and arrogant people. They were so pleased with their city and so satisfied with their progress that they would never admit that any improvement was possible. 'We are the lords of all creation,' they said loftily, 'and all people must obey us. There is no city like ours in all the world.'

One day a group of ragged Indians arrived in the city. Although they looked poor, they soon began to attract attention to themselves by prophesying that the city would be destroyed. 'Prepare,' they told the people, 'for ruin will come by earthquake and flood and fire. The smell of death is on this city!'

'What nonsense,' scoffed the city people. 'Why don't you go away? We are the greatest of all people. Look at our buildings. There are none like them in the world. Look at our water system and irrigation. Where will you find any to equal them? We are a modern, progressive race: we know how to deal with floods and earthquakes. Go away with your old wives' tales.'

The ragged band of Indians persisted in their warnings and eventually, tired of their nagging, depressing voices, the city people had them flogged and thrown out of the city. Only the priests were anxious.

'These were holy men,' they said, 'and who knows, they may be right. Perhaps they can see further than we can.'

Some of the priests took the Indians' words so seriously that they, too, left the city and retired to their temple on the hill. There they lived as hermits, cutting themselves off from the city people completely.

'Look at them,' mocked the city people. 'What good do they think they are doing up there? All they can do is preach, they've never done an honest day's work in their lives. If anyone is doomed it is they. That hill is the very place for lightning to strike. How we'll laugh when that happens.'

Then, one peaceful afternoon, one of the city people saw a small red cloud on the horizon. At first he could not tell whether it was a real cloud or just a puff of smoke from a burning house but it grew larger and larger. Soon it was obvious that it was a real cloud and that there were others massing together with it, red clouds and dark clouds the colour of lead. When night came there was no darkness, for the sky and the earth below were lit up by a glaring red light from the clouds. An eerie silence hung over the whole land.

Suddenly, there was a flash and a rumble, then an ear-splitting crash as the earth jolted violently. Many of the buildings stood firm, for they had been well constructed of stone but almost immediately a red rain started to pour from the clouds and the earth shook again, more violently even than before. Building after building crashed to the ground and the red rain grew to a continual cloudburst . . . The carefully constructed water and irrigation systems were completely destroyed; mountain rivers were jolted from their courses and a great flood rose over the buildings of the city.

Today the great Lake of Titicaca covers the proud city. Not one of its mocking inhabitants survived and it is said that some died with their unbelieving smiles still on their faces. Only the priests in their humble straw huts were saved. Their temple on the hill stood firm against the earthquake and the hill itself rose above the flood waters. Today it is the Island of the Sun.

The ragged prophets, too, survived for they watched sadly from a high place as the waters rose and the city was destroyed. Some of their descendants became the Callawayas, the wise men of the valleys by the Altiplano, travelling doctors and healers famous for their skills.

The sons of thunder

Many different tribes lived in the great Inca empire and each had its own beliefs in a god of rain and thunder. For some he was a creator god, who released the human race from the earth by turning up a spade of gold. He produced the thunder and lightning with a sling and the stones he hurled landed as thunderbolts or thunderstones which were highly valued. These were believed to bring fertility to the fields and to give protection from lightning. They were also used as love charms.

Under the Incas, the different thunder gods were unified into an important deity who was considered next in importance after the Creator and Sun gods and had a temple dedicated to him in Cuzco. A statue of him there shows an outsize human figure, his head hidden in a head-dress which symbolized the thunderclouds.

Stories about the thunder gods are still told among the Quechua Indians today. Thunder and lightning are believed to be a person who lives in the sky, sometimes referred to as an old woman, sometimes as Mamaqocha or the Great Lake. There are three sons of Thunder, the Older, the Middle and the Younger One. The oldest speaks with the loud, roaring roll of approaching thunder; the middle is more moderate, with a more distant, grumbling voice; the younger is fierce and angry, and his voice splits the sky. The three brothers occupy themselves with stealing crops—beans, potatoes and maize—and carrying them away to their own barns. People killed by lightning are also carried away to the place where food and the animals of thunder are kept and there they are used as labourers. It is said that they have plenty of food to eat but that they are among the accursed. Once, a man was lucky enough to escape . . .

A stranger was once walking through the fields when it began to rain. Night was approaching and, suspecting that a storm was on the way, he was relieved to see the light of a small hut in the distance. When he reached it he knocked at the door and a little old woman came out, white haired and bent with age.
'Let me stay the night, mamita,' said the stranger.
'I can't,' she replied. 'My sons are mad and when they return they will kill you.'
'Where can I go?' begged the stranger. 'Please let me stay.'

At last she relented and showed him to a corner of the room. 'You can stay here as long as you keep quite still. I'll cover you with a blanket and perhaps you will be safe.'

Outside the rain came down more heavily and, as the stranger had expected, it started to thunder. At first the noise was far away but it grew gradually louder and closer until it seemed that the claps of thunder were calling at the front door, 'Crack, crack, crack.' Right in the middle of the loudest crash, a man entered. The woman greeted him as her oldest son and he put his sling down on the floor. Again the thunder roared and the door opened to admit a second man. He, too, laid his sling on the floor and sat down beside it. The woman greeted him as her second son. When the thunder crashed for the third time, the youngest son entered, snarling and grumbling: 'Some wretched crop guard has been trying to smoke me out with paraffin—me, who always

steal everything! But he has paid . . .'

The stranger peeped through a hole in the blanket and saw that the youngest son had brought with him heaps of ripe maize and bundles of potatoes, beans and grain, all loaded onto the backs of mules. As he watched he saw that the ropes which tied the bundles to the mules were snakes, writhing and twisting their tails, flicking their yellow tongues towards him . . . Burying his head in the blanket, he fell anxiously asleep.

When he awoke it was daylight again; the hut and its owners had disappeared and he was lying on the wet grass by the side of a lake.

Amaru Inca

The most densely inhabited regions of the Inca empire lay in parts of the Andes where deep ravines opened into wide, sheltered valleys. Each valley was isolated from the next by harsh desert country and the people had little contact with anyone from outside their own area. A Spanish traveller, Pedro Cieza de León, described them when he visited Peru only fifteen years after the conquest, in the middle of the sixteenth century: 'As these valleys are closed in, they are not molested by the winds, nor does the snow reach them, and the land is so fruitful that all things which are sown yield abundantly; and there are trees and many birds and animals . . . There are populous villages, and rivers of excellent water flow near them; some of the rivers send their waters to the South Sea, entering by the sandy deserts which I have mentioned, and the humidity of their water gives rise to very beautiful valleys with great rows of trees. The valleys are two or three leagues broad, and great quantities of algoroba trees grow in them, which flourish even at great distances from any water. Wherever there are groves of trees the land is free from sand and very fertile and abundant . . . To prepare their fields for sowing, they lead channels from the rivers to irrigate the valleys, and the channels are made so well and with so much regularity that all the land is irrigated without any waste. This system of irrigation makes the valleys very green and cheerful, and they are full of fruit-trees. At all

times they raise good harvests of maize and wheat, and of everything that they sow.'

The story of Amaru Inca is set in one of these valleys, where the water supply and effective irrigation were vital to the life of the tribe.

There was once a tribe called the Amaru who lived in a fertile valley and were well known for the high quality of the maize and vegetables they produced. An old man named Amaru Inca was their chieftain and he had four beautiful daughters. Many young men came as suitors to the girls but the father would not allow them to marry; he had decided to send them to the Temple of the Sun in Cuzco to serve the Sun God and the chief Inca.

One day, before the girls had left for Cuzco, a new suitor arrived.

'I came from the valley of Waman,' he said, 'far away in the high mountains. Before I came here I made sacrifices to the mountain gods. I made offerings too, to the Earth Mother, Pachamama, and she told me that what I am doing is right. So, listen, sir, to what I have to say. If you allow me to marry your oldest daughter, both your family and mine will join to become a powerful and prosperous tribe.'

The young man spoke eloquently but Amaru Inca was not impressed. With his eyes flashing, he thundered, 'Get out of my sight, young man. You talk as if you are trading in goats and llamas. My daughters are worth far more than anything your people can offer. So go, quickly, before I lose my temper.'

The young man went angrily away and told the mountain spirits of his humiliation. He told the Earth Mother, Pachamama, that she had deceived him. Then he went to the three lakes which supplied water to the Amaru valley and asked them to avenge his dishonour.

Throwing three handfuls of sand into each of the lakes, he cried, 'Avenge my humiliation, O lakes. Let the Amaru and their land be dry and withered. Let the crops fail and the people go hungry.'

When the young man returned home and explained what had happened, his father, too, was enraged at the insult and he ordered that the passage from Amaru to the next fertile valley should be blockaded so that no-one could pass

through. Very soon, the Amaru people began to feel the effects of the young man's curse. Streams and rivers dried up and the sun beat down on the growing plants, withering their leaves and shrivelling the fruits before they were ripe. Eventually the people met together to try to discover what was causing the drought and it was only then that they learned about the old man's treatment of the man from Waman. They decided finally to visit the three lakes themselves and they made their way to the head of the valley. To their surprise, they discovered that two of the lakes had dried up completely while the streams that had flowed from the third were blocked with heaps of sand and rock. At once they began to dig a new canal so that the water could flow from the lake again; today the river they released is still the only one that waters their valley and is named Viejo Amaru (Old Man Amaru) as a record of the old chieftain's pride.

Once they had restored their water supply, the men of Amaru marched into the valley of Waman to attack the people who had so nearly brought disaster. There were several angry skirmishes in which men from both sides were wounded but eventually the men of Amaru returned to their own valley. To this day there is a bitter quarrel between the two valleys but the experience had a lasting influence on the people of Amaru. While in other villages, marriage with strangers from a neighbouring valley is frowned upon, in Amaru, it is considered unlucky to refuse.

The snake sister

There was once an unmarried woman who had no children and who lived alone, quite contented with her position in life. One day she was working in her garden when she saw a snake. She jumped back in alarm but the snake did not attack her, it merely lay looking at her intently. She thought it was a very odd shape and decided that it looked pregnant.

'How strange,' she said to herself, but the snake eventually slithered away and she forgot all about it until the next morning when to her surprise she discovered that she was pregnant herself.

All that day she remained in the house, too frightened to stir outside. When she went to bed at night she was unable to sleep for a long time, but tossed and turned restlessly. At last she drifted into sleep, only to find herself dreaming vividly about the snake. In the dream the snake was able to speak to her and she was talking to it about her condition.

'It was I who made you pregnant,' hissed the snake, coiling around her feet. 'It was I.' Then the woman woke up.

Before many months had passed, the woman gave birth to twins. To her horror, only one of them was a human daughter: the other was a snake. Again, the poor woman was frantic with worry and again it was a dream that gave her an answer. While she dozed fitfully one evening, rocking the human daughter in her arms, the snake child appeared to her in a dream. Like the first snake, it could talk the woman's own language.

'Mother,' hissed the snake child pleadingly, 'I will never thrive in the house like my twin sister. Put me back in the garden, in the same place where you met the snake before. There I was conceived and there I must return.'

Naturally the woman was relieved to have found a way of disposing of the snake child and the very next morning she took it out to the garden and put it down among the maize. At once it slithered away under the leaves and silently disappeared.

The woman and her daughter lived together happily for many years and the child grew up to

61

be a beautiful woman. For a long time she refused to leave her mother and get married and she turned down many of the local young men who asked for her hand. Eventually, however, a man from a distant village came to live nearby and within a short time they had decided to become husband and wife. They had been together for some time when the man announced that he was going to visit his family.

'I will go first to tell them about our marriage and then return to collect you,' he said. 'You cannot travel alone.'

The husband set off. As he disappeared into the distance, the young wife heard a slithering noise and felt something brush against her bare feet. Looking down she saw a snake and to her surprise it spoke to her.

'Your husband will come back with a good horse to carry you on,' it said, 'but you must on no account ride it; instead you must travel on a little donkey. You'll find one tethered nearby when the time comes. Be sure to take with you some cotton thread, some soap, a comb, some wool and a pair

of scissors. And be sure to travel at the back of the group.'

The wife knew nothing about her strange snake sister but she could not disregard advice from such a mysterious source, even if she did not understand it. When her husband duly came back for his wife, sure enough he had a handsome horse all ready for her to ride. The wife made quite a fuss.

'No. I'll not ride on that large animal, he looks too frisky for me. Look, there's a donkey tethered over there. That's more suitable for me. I'll ride on that.'

The husband saw that she was determined, so he helped her up onto the donkey and led it to the front of the group of people who were travelling with them. Again the wife protested, 'No, no, I can't travel in the front, my donkey will only hold you all up. Let me ride at the back where we won't be in the way.'

Before the party set off, the wife made sure she had hidden all the things the snake had told her to in her saddle bag.

They had travelled for some hours and the wife was growing tired, when they came to a farm. At first she was pleased at the thought of food and rest but as they approached the farmhouse, she experienced a strong feeling of foreboding. Suddenly the door of the farmhouse opened a crack and she caught a glimpse of what lay inside. Shuddering with fear, she realized her husband had brought her to the door of hell itself. Without a word, she turned her donkey round, kicked it urgently in the side and galloped away.

The husband was at the head of the column of travellers, while the wife had travelled all the way at the rear, so she had a head start in her flight. However, his horse was far more powerful than her little donkey and before long she could hear its hooves pounding along behind her. Looking fearfully over her shoulder, she saw that her husband had taken on a new and horrible form: he was the devil itself.

'Oh please go faster,' she urged the donkey, but though it was willing, it could not outstrip their pursuer and the large horse behind drew steadily nearer and nearer.

In her panic, she remembered the advice of her snake sister. This must be what she had foreseen.

Without really knowing what she was doing, she reached in the saddle bag, drew out the pieces of cotton thread and threw them onto the path behind her. As they fluttered down, they turned into strands of mist, twining together thickly, bringing darkness into the day. As the mist spread out, the hoof-beats of the horse behind her faded away. She had hardly time to sigh with relief, however, when the sounds drew relentlessly nearer again. Next she threw down the pieces of soap she had brought. Immediately, the soap became heavy rain, turning the path into a slippery torrent and forcing the husband to fall back once more. Again she thought she had escaped him but again he drew nearer. This time she dropped the comb, which turned into a thorny tangle of undergrowth, holding him up for a while. But before long he was drawing nearer again.

By this time the woman was very near her own home—but her husband the devil was so close she could hear his horrible breathing. Desperately she threw down the skein of wool and was relieved to see a thick forest spring up, the great trees standing so close together that there was hardly room to squeeze between them. The wife was almost at her gate when she dared to look back again, only to see her husband's hand reaching for the donkey's tufted tail. The only thing she had left now in her saddle bag was a pair of scissors and, though she could not imagine what use they could be, she threw them towards her pursuer. Immediately a great calm and silence descended. The hoof-beats behind her ceased; the furious cries of pursuit died away. Even her heart seemed to stop thumping so loudly. Turning round, she saw that the scissors had turned into a tall green cross which stood between her and the devil. Quite unable to pass it, her husband cringed back into the darkness and disappeared into the night.

Dismounting, the wife led the donkey into her garden and patted its nose. As she did so, the donkey changed before her eyes into a coiling snake—her snake sister had been with her all along.

'Be careful who you marry, next time,' said the sister. 'Whatever you do, don't marry a stranger. Take someone you know.'

And she slid away into the grass.

Ollantay and the Inca

The story of Ollantay is told in a play which was first written down in the eighteenth century, but is probably based on a far more ancient drama. Forty-five miles north of Cuzco stands the great fortress of Ollantaytambo, perched on a cliff and surrounded by great walls and stone terraces where maize may have been cultivated. It may originally have been named after a famous chieftain and the play may have once told his story. In the Inca version, the chief character is a general in the army of the Inca Pachacutec.

Ollantay was a just man and a courageous fighter, loved by all the people. As a famous and valued general he naturally came into contact with the Inca and his family and he was unfortunate enough to fall in love with the Inca's daughter Cusi-Coyllur. The name Cusi-Coyllur means 'star' and she was indeed as beautiful as the brightest star in the heavens. Ollantay's love was unfortunate because, even for such an important man as Ollantay, to think of marrying the Inca's daughter was impossible. In Inca law no-one might marry out of his or her predetermined and unchangeable position in society.

However brave Ollantay was, however many trophies he had won in battle, however many lands he had conquered for his emperor—all this was of no importance. Even the fact that Cusi Coyllur loved him in return made no difference. Naturally, it made Ollantay very happy to know that she loved him, but at the same time he was filled with despair because he did not know what to do.

One day they went together to the high priest, Willac-Uma, a venerable and sympathetic old man. They told him that since there seemed to be no way out of their problem, they had decided to get married secretly. The old man was aghast: 'You can't do that!' he said. 'You of all people should know that you are committing sacrilege. The Inca is a god and all his family are gods, too. You, Ollantay, are a mortal and even to think of marrying a god is a terrible sin.'
'It can't be wrong to love each other as we do,' said Cusi Coyllur, 'not really wrong. Even if the laws say we should not marry, I cannot believe it is a sin.'
'I know what you mean,' said the old man gently, 'but the laws of this land are strict and it is by being strict that we have grown great and powerful. It is only by obeying the law that we remain strong.'

In spite of the old man's advice, the couple decided they could not obey the laws of the empire and a few days later they were married very quietly without anyone knowing.

One day, some months later, Cusi-Coyllur said to Ollantay, 'Why don't we ask my father ourselves? He is getting old and I don't like to deceive him in this way. Perhaps he will relent and forget the laws of the Incas when he sees how happy we are.'

Ollantay agreed, though he felt very uneasy about it, and they went together before the Inca—not to confess their secret marriage outright but to prepare the way for such a surprise by explaining what they wanted to do.

When Pachacutec heard Ollantay's request, he became very angry.

'Don't you know your place, man?' he roared. 'You may be a famous soldier but you are still the Inca's vassal and that will never change. What you suggest is quite out of the question. I shall have Cusi-Coyllur shut away in the temple of Acllahuasi, the house of the priestesses of the Sun. There she shall be guarded by the holy women, safe from your unlawful intentions. As for you, return to your quarters immediately.'

Neither Ollantay nor Cusi-Coyllur dared to say any more about their attachment; even less did they wish to confess that they were already secretly married and that in fact Cusi-Coyllur was expecting a child. They knew that if they told the truth now, they would both certainly be put to death. So, sadly, they bowed and left the Inca's presence, Ollantay being shown to a door which led to the army quarters, Cusi-Coyllur to another which led to the Temple of the Sun.

Cusi-Coyllur was treated well by the holy women and several months later she gave birth to a daughter. She named her Ima-Sumac, which means 'the very beautiful one'. The child was taken from her immediately and brought up in a separate part of the temple.

Unable to see his wife or learn anything about

her, Ollantay himself grew desperate. He could not believe that he had done anything wrong; he knew from his own experience that social rank of itself did not separate people in any real way and, brooding for long hours in his quarters, he came to the conclusion that the great laws of the Inca empire were unjust. To make his position clear, he decided to rebel against Pachacutec: only in this way would he have any chance of seeing Cusi-Coyllur again. With a band of faithful soldiers, he marched on the great fortress of Ollantaytambo in the Sacred Valley of the Incas.

Ollantay's forces defeated the Inca's army in a great battle and the rebels occupied the fortress. However, the Inca's general, Ruminawi or 'Eye of the Stone' was an astute man and he thought of a way of defeating Ollantay by cunning. Pretending to be a disaffected member of the Inca's army who was taking refuge with the rebels, he made his way to the fortress and begged for Ollantay's protection. Ollantay ordered the great gates of the fortress to be opened and Ruminawi was allowed to enter. The soldiers were all exhausted from their hard days fighting and as night came, they fell asleep, secure inside the locked gates. Ruminawi waited until the last of them was safely snoring, then stole down and opened the gates to let in the Inca's army, who, as he had ordered, had silently assembled outside. Within minutes they had overpowered Ollantay's sleepy followers and it was all over. Ollantay and his lieutenant Urco Waranca were bound in chains and escorted back to the capital, Cuzco, some forty-five miles away.

They had not travelled far when the group of manacled prisoners and their guards saw a cloud of dust in the distance.
'Unless I'm mistaken, that is one of the royal runners,' said Ruminawi to the soldier beside him. 'That must mean important news.'

Ollantay did not look up; he was too worried, preoccupied with the thought of the dishonourable death that awaited him in Cuzco. What would happen to Cusi-Coyllur now? Had she had her baby? Would his child be allowed to survive? Above all, he thought over and over again, why did I rebel against the Inca? How can a soldier defeat a god? Then, through his thoughts, he heard the breathless voice of the runner:

'Greetings O Ruminawi, and to you, too, noble prisoner Ollantay. I am the bearer of sad news. Our Inca Pachacutec died early today. All the court is in mourning. His son Tupac Yupanqui has succeeded the great Inca and will receive the prisoners tomorrow.'

Ollantay felt even more filled with foreboding. What would his reception be like now? Surely his rebellion would be blamed for the death of a beloved emperor.

All the way to Cuzco, Ollantay brooded on his situation and next day, in his prison cell, he was still trying to gather his thoughts. He had known the young Inca Tupac Yupanqui all his life; he was the brother of his beloved wife; but he could not guess how he would feel about the law of the Incas, about which Pachacutec had been so strict.

At midday, when the sun was at its highest point in the sky, the prisoner Ollantay was led before the new Inca. There was a long silence as Ollantay stood before him and Tupac Yupanqui seemed to be thinking deeply. Finally he spoke. 'Ollantay, you are here before me as a prisoner, as a rebel against my father and the laws of the Inca. My grief at seeing you in such a position, you of all men, a general and champion of my armies, is without bounds. From being among the mightiest of men you have fallen to be a wretched traitor, one whom justice would hang from the nearest tree without any further thought.'
'True, O Inca,' replied Ollantay humbly.
'Everything you say is true and I do not deny it. And I would do it again. I had nothing against your father, whom I loved as I loved my own parents. My quarrel is with the Inca law that says that one man may be a god, another a mere human and that the two may not join hands.'
'But the empire is held together by its traditions and its laws,' said the young Inca. 'You have fought yourself to maintain it.'
'No empire can be held together by unjust laws, only by those its people feel to be just. Those laws which forbid men to walk together are against true justice and the Inca state can only exist in spite of them, not because of them. The greatness of the Inca comes not from laws alone, but from his faith and his fortitude.'
The young Inca rose to his feet. 'You have put into words what I have always felt,' he said, 'but I

wanted to hear it from you rather than to say it myself. From henceforth you shall have your honours and titles back and be again a free man. My pardon be with you.' Turning to his advisers, the Inca said, 'Bring my sister Cusi-Coyllur from the temple of the priestesses of the Sun and give her to this man. Ollantay, from now on Cusi-Coyllur shall be your official wife and the daughter she has borne you shall be your true daughter.'

So ends the story of Ollantay and Cusi-Coyllur, who settled down together in the Inca capital Cuzco and founded a famous family which served the empire for many years.

The girl from the sky

There was once a man who grew the best potatoes in all the land. Many types of potato grew in those days but he alone knew how to grow this outstanding variety. Unfortunately, his patch of land was plagued by robbers who came every night to pull up the plants and steal the wonderful food.

One day the man called his only son and told him, 'It is not right that with a young strong son like you around the house we cannot defend ourselves from thieves. Go and keep watch over our crop. Sleep beside the field and catch the robbers red-handed.'

The first night the young man stayed awake all night long, peering through the darkness at the neat rows of potato plants. Only as daylight returned, did he fall fast asleep, overcome by tiredness. He was asleep for only a few minutes but in that instant the robbers came and when he awoke, he saw that several rows of plants had been devastated. Rather ashamedly he returned home and confessed what had happened. 'We'll forgive you this time. But go back tonight and keep better guard,' said his parents.

That night the young man tried even harder to stay awake but just at midnight his eyes drooped for no more than a second. In that instant, the robbers raided the field and, though he watched again until daybreak, he saw no sign of them at all. More ashamed than ever, he told his parents, 'I

watched all night for the robbers but when I shut my eyes for no more than a second at midnight, they came.'

'Do you really expect us to believe that the robbers came while you were watching? I suppose you were off chasing the girls and enjoying yourself instead of sitting in the field.' And they gave him a beating to teach him to stay at his post.

That night the young man returned to his task. From the moment he arrived at the edge of the field he was watchful, motionless and alert. There was a bright moon and he could see every plant clearly but as the moon set and the first light of dawn appeared in the east, his eyelids trembled with fatigue and for a few seconds he dozed off again. In that fleeting moment of sleep the field was suddenly full of a multitude of beautiful, fair-skinned young women. Their faces were like flowers, their hair shone like gold and they were dressed all in silver, for they were star people from the sky. Working swiftly together, the girls started to dig up the potatoes.

When the young man's tired eyes opened again, he thought he must be dreaming for the girls were still there, busily digging and collecting the potatoes. 'How can people as lovely as this stoop to such a low task?' he wondered. Then, 'How can I catch them? If only I could take one of these beautiful people for my own...'

Leaping from his hiding place, he ran among the girls, trying to grab their hands, their clothes, anything which he could hold on to. As they scattered, he managed to catch one by her long, fair hair and, as the rest rose into the sky like fading sparks, he held her firmly.

'So it was you who stole my father's crops, was it?' he said angrily.

The star girl said nothing and the young man looked into her eyes, seeing how beautiful and afraid she was.

'Stay with me and be my wife,' he pleaded, forgetting all about the lost potato plants. 'Please stay.' And he led her towards a hut at the edge of the field.

'Let me go, let me go,' cried the star girl. 'My sisters will tell my parents. I promise to give back all the potatoes we have stolen. Don't force me to live on earth. I shall die here.'

The young man was deaf to the lovely girl's pleas. He kept a firm hold of her hand and, deciding not to return to his parents' house, he stayed with the star girl in the hut, close by the field.

Meanwhile, the young man's parents were wondering what had happened to him. 'The idiot has allowed the potatoes to be stolen again,' they said. 'It is the only possible reason why he does not show his face here.'

As time passed and still the young man did not return, the mother decided to take some food to him in the fields and find out what he was doing. The young man and the star girl saw her walking up the path and the girl said, 'You must not let her see me. No-one must know I am here.'

The young man ran out to meet his mother, calling out to her while she was still some way off, 'No mother, don't come any closer! Wait for me there!' But as he took the food from her to share with the star girl, he whispered to her everything that had happened, and, of course, as soon as the mother returned home, she in turn passed the news to her husband.

The young man tried to persuade the star girl to go home with him but she was determined. 'Your parents must never see me,' she insisted. 'Nothing good will come of it.' Eventually, however, he tricked her into walking with him to their house and, much against her wishes, he introduced her to his parents.

The parents received her with gentle amazement. She was so radiant and beautiful that she seemed to bring light to the house and they looked after her well and grew fond of her. However, they took away her silver clothes as a precaution and never allowed her out of the house, so that no-one else suspected her existence.

The star girl remained on earth for several months, but she never accepted her fate and continued to be sad and forlorn. Then one day, when the young man was working far from the house, she persuaded the mother to allow her to try on her silver clothes once more.
'I am sure it will make me happier,' she said sadly and the mother, hoping to make her more satisfied with her situation, unlocked the chest where the clothes were kept. As soon as the star

girl was wearing her own clothes again, her face became radiant once more. While the mother stood gazing in new admiration, she slipped unhindered through the door and sped away, back to the sky kingdom.

When the young man returned, he was wild with grief. He wandered off into the mountains, searching for his wife, his mind deranged with weeping until, on a high and lonely peak, he met a great condor.

'Why are you grieving?' asked the condor and the young man told his story.

'The most beautiful woman in the world was mine. Now she is gone, and I don't know where to find her. I am afraid she has fled back to the sky kingdom and I shall never see her again.'

When he had finished, the condor replied, 'Don't weep, young man. It is true she has returned to the sky, but I can see your misery is great and if you want me to, I will take you to that other world. All I ask is that you bring me two llamas. One to eat here and the other for the journey.'

'Very well, sir,' answered the young man. 'I will bring you the two llamas you have asked for. Please, I beg you, wait for me here.' He ran home straight away in search of the llamas and when he arrived, he said to his parents, 'Father, mother, I'm going to search for my wife. I have found someone who can take me to where she is. All he asks for in payment for so great a favour are two llamas.'

He took the two llamas for the condor and the great bird devoured one immediately, tearing the flesh with its beak and crunching up even the bones. With the young man's help, it slaughtered the other to eat on the journey. It ordered the young man to shoulder the carcass and climb on a rock, then took him on to its back and gave him this warning: 'You must shut your eyes tightly and under no circumstances must you open them. Every time I say "meat" you must place a piece of llama meat in my beak. If you fail, I shall let you fall.' With that, the condor took to the air.

The young man obeyed and did not open his eyes for a single moment; indeed, he kept them very tightly shut. 'Meat,' called the condor after a time, and the young man cut great chunks of llama meat and placed them in the condor's beak. The

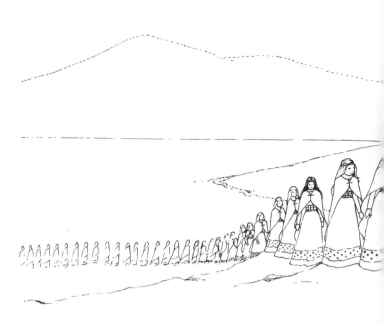

journey went on and on until, just at the highest point, the food ran out. The young man was so frightened of falling from the condor's back that he began to cut pieces off his own calf, and now every time the condor asked for meat he gave him small pieces of his own flesh. Thus, at the cost of his own blood, he enabled the condor to reach the sky kingdom.

They say that the journey took a whole year to complete and that when they arrived at last in the sky kingdom, both were dirty, wrinkled and aged. The condor rested for a moment, then led the young man to the shores of a lake. Together they bathed in the water and when they came out again, they were handsome and young.

Then the condor said to the young man, 'On the other shore of this lake there is a great temple, where a ceremony is about to be performed. Go and wait in the doorway, for all the girls of the sky will attend the ceremony. There are countless numbers of them and they all look like your wife. When they pass by you, do not speak to any of them. Your wife will be among the last to pass by, and she will touch you with her arm. Then you must grab hold of her as firmly as you can. Don't let go for any reason.'

The young man obeyed the condor and made his way to the great temple of the Sun and Moon,

the father and mother of the stars. There he waited by the doorway as an endless stream of identical star girls filed in to perform their daily ceremonies. On they came, one after the other, each one glancing impassively at the intruder. He could not tell which one might be his wife but as the last few were going past, one of them touched him gently with her elbow before entering the temple with the rest. He tried to catch her, but she was too quick for him.

When the ceremony was over, the star girls began to come out again and still the young man waited by the door. Again, they looked at him with indifference and again he could not tell one from the other. Then one of them touched him with her elbow and, this time, before she could escape, he held her by the arm.

'Why have you come all this way?' she asked. 'I was coming back to you.'

But the young man did not believe her and as he refused to let her go, she led him to her house. By the time they arrived there, he was shivering with cold and hunger and the star girl fed him with soup made from quinoa grains and hid him from her parents.

'They must never see you,' she explained, 'or they will send us both away.'

For a whole year the young man lived in hiding in the star girl's house. She brought him food every day and cared for him lovingly. Then, one day she said, 'Your place is on the earth, not here in the sky. The time has come for you to go. I shall never see you again.'

That night he waited in vain for her to return; but she had left him forever. The young man knew that he, too, must go and, sadly, he made his way to the shores of the lake. There he saw the condor gliding high above him and as soon as it saw him, it swooped down to meet him. When the condor landed the young man saw that, once again, it looked old and tired. The condor for its part saw an old, sad man instead of the young husband it had left the year before.

'What's happened?' it asked and the man told his story, sighing.

'My poor friend, how could she treat you like that?' said the condor, coming closer and stroking him gently with its great wings.

'Sir, lend me your wings once more and take me back to my father's house,' said the man.

'Very well,' the condor replied, 'but first let us bathe once more in the lake.'

As before, the waters of the lake made both man and bird young and strong again, ready to undertake the great journey to the earth. 'You will have to give me two llamas in return for the use of my wings,' said the condor.

'Sir, when we get home, I will give you as many llamas as you wish,' replied the young man.

A year later, the journey was over and the young man returned to his parents' house. Overcome with grief at losing their only son, they had grown old but their spirits leaped when they saw him safe and sound.

The condor was quickly rewarded for its kindness with two llamas and the little family settled down together. From time to time the parents tried to persuade their son to take a wife, to give them grandchildren and bring life and happiness back to their home, but he always replied, 'I can love no other woman but the star girl. I shall never find anyone like her and so I will live alone here till death comes to claim me.'

Understanding his sorrow, they cared for him as best they could and so he lived out his days, with a great sadness in his heart, remembering the beautiful star girl who had been his wife.

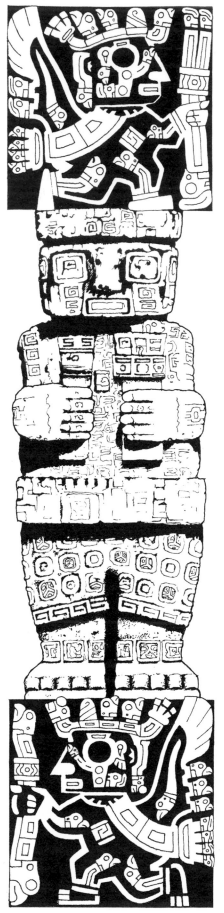

Myths of the high Andes

The area around Lake Titicaca, the great lake which lies on the high plateau of Peru and Bolivia, is known as the Collao. The ruins of the city of Tiahuanaco which stand at its southern end are the remains of what may once have been a great empire and the people called the Colla who now live in the area are probably the descendants of a tribe who were powerful long before the Incas ruled.

The Colla were among the most difficult of people for the Incas to defeat. Already highly civilized, they resented the Incas as upstarts, especially when the Incas claimed that they had come from the islands of the Sun and Moon in Lake Titicaca—islands which the Colla themselves considered sacred.

When one race conquers another their myths and legends often become mixed and this happened with the Colla and the Incas. The name of Viracocha, the Inca Creator god, was often confused with Thunupa, the Colla god of Thunder and Lightning and was also linked with Kon-Tiki, the Creator god of the Colla.

It was the name Kon-Tiki that led the Norwegian scientist Thor Heyerdahl to suggest that people from what is now Peru and Bolivia crossed the Pacific Ocean to Polynesia a thousand years ago or more. For Tiki is also the name of a sun god from Easter Island, a god who seems similar in many ways to the Colla's Kon-Tiki. According to one Colla legend, when the god Kon-Tiki had created man, he travelled northwards and later crossed the ocean, walking on the waves. Was this perhaps a memory of a real expedition?

The names of Tiki and Kon-Tiki are not the only similarities Thor Heyerdahl found. On both Easter Island and at Tiahuanaco there are giant stone statues and in both countries they have similar belts carved around their stomachs, traditional emblems of the Sun god. The Easter Island statues have long-lobed ears and the Colla were known as 'long ears' because they artificially lengthened their ear lobes. The Polynesians use knotted strings, like Inca *quipus*, for calculating. In some cases even place names are similar.

Thor Heyerdahl took his list to leading scholars but they refused to be convinced. They said that the people of the Andes were not seafarers and had no ships capable of crossing the Pacific. As an answer, Heyerdahl built a balsa wood raft, using only materials the Indians would have used, and in 1947, with five companions, he successfully made the 4,000-mile ocean crossing to Easter Island. He named the raft the *Kon-Tiki*.

We may never know whether his theory is correct, but at least he had proved that the great journey could have happened.

The stone men

The giant stone statues that still stand at Tiahuanaco, Pucara and in several other places in Peru and Bolivia are among the great mysteries of the South American continent. Many theories have been used to explain their presence, including Thor Heyerdahl's; even during Inca times they were considered ancient and were treated with reverence and awe.

The Indians who lived in the country around had many legends which told how the statues had been made. The Incas believed that their Creator God, Viracocha, had made them first as a race of giants who rebelled against him and were turned to stone as a punishment. The Colla had a similar story but believed that stone men were prototypes of humankind.

Long ago, they said, the great Lord Kon-Tiki emerged from the cold Lake Titicaca with a band of followers and settled in a place called Tiahuanaco. There he made the Sun and the Moon and there he decided to make a new race of people to replace the giants who had turned against him. This time all went well.

First, Kon-Tiki made carved stone statues of all the people he wanted to create. He made leaders and warriors, he made men who could plough and work in the fields, he made women who could bear children and he made babies in their rush cradles. He made their features and their clothing and painted them in the colours they would wear. Then he turned to his followers: 'These are the models of the future people of this land. Listen while I name each one and when I have named each one and decided where each shall live, you, my helpers, will carry them with you to the caves, wells and springs from which their living images will appear.'

Kon-Tiki's followers at once went out all over the country with the stone statues and placed them in the positions they had been shown. Then Kon-Tiki called out loudly, 'Come forth', and in all the different regions, men, women and children appeared, leaders and farmers and warriors, all in the pattern of the stone statues.

When Kon-Tiki was satisfied that all was well, he took two companions and travelled north until, just beyond Cuzco, he was challenged by a hostile tribe, the Canas. The Canas attacked Kon-Tiki with spears but the Creator's power was far too great for them. In a moment he had called a hail of fire onto their heads, while in the distance a mountain exploded with unimaginable force, sending a shower of stones onto the ground around them. The terrified Canas prostrated themselves and Kon-Tiki extinguished the fire with a single blow of his stick, commanding the mountain to be silent at the same time.

The Canas accepted him as their god and built a shrine or *huaca* to him in the place where the fire had appeared. According to an early Spanish traveller in Peru, the shrine was still in existence, together with a great stone figure of Kon-Tiki. To the left of the shrine, the land was scarred and burned for almost a mile, and was littered with stones which, the Indians told him, were the very stones which had rained down on their ancestors who challenged the great Lord Kon-Tiki.

The origin of coca

For the Indians who lived high on the Altiplano, life must always have been a continuous struggle. The climate is harsh and the soil poor, barely covering the rock in some places. To the east, the peaks of the Andes rise thousands of metres into the thin, cold air.

Long ago, no-one knew what lay on the other side of the mountain range.
'I have heard that when the gods created the Altiplano and the mountains where they live, they had no earth left to make any more land. On the other side of the mountains there is nothing but air,' said one man.
'True,' said another, 'but I have also heard that if

you can cling to the side of the mountain at the end of the world, far below there is a great green carpet where the air is hot and everything grows in abundance.'

The tribesmen looked towards the towering peaks of Illimani and Illampu with awe. What could they see when they looked towards the sunrise? At first no-one spoke, then one young man who had always had a reputation for being an adventurer said what was in everyone's mind. 'I am going to see for myself. Who will come with me?'

After a long discussion, the whole tribe decided to take the journey to the end of the world and they set out towards the mountains. For many weary days they climbed the passes, until they reached a place where the earth seemed to fall away as the land plunged down some 4,000 metres to the jungle below, to the great green zone of heat and rain which feeds the Amazon river. Slowly, they made the precarious descent. At first they were terrified by the loud noises that filled the jungle—the screams of birds, the howling of the monkeys, the roars and cries that chill the blood. How different it all was from the quietness of their frozen home. There the winds might swirl and moan but they had always their great Lake Titicaca to calm them, reflecting the mountain homes of the gods in its clear blue water. Here in the jungle the animals had taken over. They could not be touched or seen but they were everywhere, close, insistent, menacing.

'We must not be afraid,' said the oldest chief. 'Let us clear the jungle trees and make the land ready for planting. If we work hard the Sun will give us an abundant harvest.'

The tribe set to work, hacking at the thick roots, slashing the twining creepers to make a clearing where they could live. Soon it was obvious that cutting would not clear the dense tropical plants so they made a fire and set the forest alight. Clouds of thick smoke rose above the trees. Higher and higher it rose until it reached the pure snows of the mountains.

The gods of the mountains were extremely angry when they saw how their white snow was dirtied by the smoke and they decided the Indians must be punished.

'I shall send down a terrible rain and wash them all away,' announced Khuno, the god of the snow. 'They will all be exterminated.'

'Killing them is no punishment,' said the great mountain Illimani. 'Let them live but let them suffer great hardship.'

So Khuno sent a great storm which swept away everything the Indians had managed to build and grow in their small clearing, but he spared their lives. Sheltering in damp, bat-infested caves, they watched the devastation around them.

'It is the end,' said the oldest chief. 'We have nothing here and we cannot go back. We are weak with hunger and there is no food that we can eat. Let us die in these caves and leave our bones as a warning to others.'

'Don't give up,' said the young man who had first suggested the journey. 'Everything looks hopeless but there are still some trees and shrubs left here and there. Let's see whether they can give us any food.'

He stepped out of the cave, blinking in the bright sunlight which followed the storm. Immediately he saw a small shrub with brilliant green leaves. Its leaves looked so inviting and he was so hungry that he picked a handful and put them into his mouth. At once a great feeling of contentment came over him. He no longer felt hungry and he forgot the damp and discomfort all around him. Seeing the joy on his face, the other Indians followed his example and soon they were all chewing the leaves. The plant they had discovered was the coca plant.

When the people of the tribe felt well and strong again they took seeds and cuttings from the wonderful plant and made their way back to Tiahuanaco. Coca became an important part of their lives from then on. When they chewed it mixed with lime they no longer felt hungry and it seemed to give them strength and energy. Their wise men used it to foretell the future, to diagnose diseases and as a medicine. Also it was offered to the gods and spirits of the dead.

In its processed form coca is the source of the dangerous drug cocaine and there is today a thriving, if illegal trade, which smuggles it to the United States. Although governments have repeatedly tried to stamp out the actual practice of chewing the leaves, it remains very much a part of Indian life.

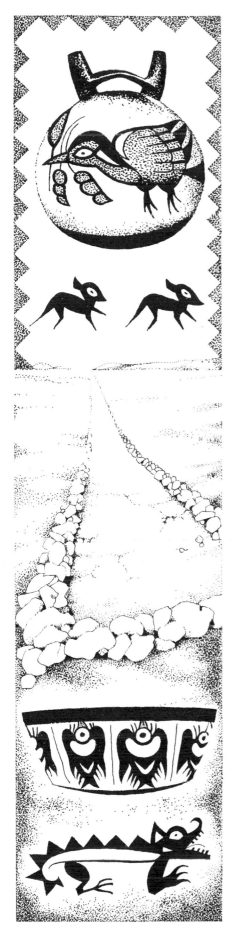

Mysteries of the valleys

The great Atacama Desert which runs down the western coast of South America from the Peruvian frontier with Ecuador to half-way down the Chilean plain, is one of the largest stretches of dry land in the world. For years at a time no rain falls at all and without irrigation, no plants can grow in the dry, stony soil. At intervals along the desert coast, however, there are valleys made fertile by rivers which flow down from the Andes and here, with careful use of the river water, agriculture is possible.

The valley oases have been inhabited for many thousands of years and fragments of pottery have been found dating back to between 3800 and 1800 BC. Between 600 and 300 BC people belonging to a culture called the Chavin were influential and their style of art, textiles and pottery are found over a large area, together with the remains of imposing temples. By AD 900 the most powerful people in the area were the Chimu, whose city of Chan Chan is the best known archaeological site in South America. Built near Trujillo in northern Peru, it covered an area of ten square miles with temples, palaces and houses for the ordinary inhabitants. The Chimu ruled over many of the neighbouring valleys and were powerful enough to organize the building of complex irrigation systems connecting one valley with the next.

The Chimu gods included the great creator Pachacamac and when the Incas finally conquered the Chimu in the early 1460s they incorporated the coastal god into their own family of deities. The ruins of his great temple still stand near the Valley of Lurin, south of Lima, built on a rock high above the ocean. Pachacamac became so important in Inca religion that the principal national feast, held at the summer solstice, was dedicated to him.

Further south lived the Nazca people, whose civilization was at its peak between 300 BC and AD 700, before the Incas began to spread through the region. When the Incas did invade, they used their engineering skills to improve irrigation enormously. By cutting deep trenches from the mountains they channelled rainwater to feed a small river which was then diverted into several branches to water a wider area than before.

Among the most fascinating of all archaeological puzzles are the

Nazca lines which mark the desert land over hundreds of square miles. They were made by removing the surface rocks and exposing the lighter underlying ground. Some are straight lines extending for over a mile; others are geometric shapes such as triangles and squares or the outlines of living things—a dog, a monkey, birds, a spider, a tree. Some scholars believe that they were made nearly three thousand years ago and, since there is no rain to disturb the ground, have remained clearly distinguishable ever since. Even the piles of stones which were removed from the surface are still piled beside the outlines.

From the ground it is impossible to see their real shapes and it was not until the 1920s, when they were first viewed from the air, that their complete outlines and complexity were finally discovered.

No-one knows how they were drawn with such accuracy, or what their real purpose was and, as with all mysteries, many theories have been put forward to explain them. Since they are only completely visible from the air, it has been suggested that they were offerings to the sky gods—and that they were identification marks to enable visiting space men to land safely! Others suggested that they were ancient roads or that they were a kind of calendar which farmers used to predict the arrival of rain. One day we may discover that they were used for religious purposes and that they have an important part to play in Nazca mythology. Meanwhile, after lying undisturbed for thousands of years, their greatest threat now comes from the eager tourists whose trampling feet easily destroy the ancient outlines.

Very different from the coastal valleys are the valleys known as the Yungas, which run down from the eastern side of the Andes ranges of the high plateau of Peru and Bolivia, dropping steeply to the great jungle lands of the Amazon basin. The plateau itself is 3,000–4,000 metres above sea level and the passes through the mountains are a thousand or more metres higher. From these the Yunga valleys fall away so steeply that the journey to the forest below can be made very quickly and many of the Yungas have become important trade routes.

The lower parts of the valleys are fertile, rich in fruit and vegetables. Oranges, bananas, and coffee all grow easily in the lush, tropical climate.

The ancient peoples knew and used them and the peoples of the high plateau told stories about the mysterious land beyond the mountains which contrasted so strongly with their own harsher environment.

People have always moved from the highlands in two directions—towards the coast with its city cultures and valley oases and towards the hot, fertile jungle to the east. Today the Bolivian and Peruvian governments are trying to encourage settlers to move eastwards rather than to crowd into the already densely populated cities such as La Paz and Lima.

According to legend, however, there was a time when people from the coast moved inland to settle in the mountain valleys. The story of the walking idols, told by the people of the Yungas, may be a half remembered account of the movements and conquests of different tribes in the far distant past.

The giants

Hundreds of years ago, they say, a group of giant strangers landed on the desolate coast of northern Peru, near where the town of Portoviejo stands today.

The giants arrived in boats made of balsa wood, great boats as big as ocean sailing ships. The men were so large that an ordinary man would reach no higher than their knees. Their eyes were as large as plates and their hair reached to their powerful shoulders, though they wore no beards. Their clothes were made of animal skins and some went naked. There were no women with them and no children.

As soon as they landed they began to search for water and, finding no easy supply, they started to dig deep into the rock. Far down under the desert they found hidden wells and springs where the water was clear and cold, tasting fresh and clean. The giants made their wells to last, lining them with stone and building stone cisterns where the water could collect in large quantities. Then they built their village and settled down to stay.

The giants were not warlike people but their

effect on the country around was almost as disastrous as war; they devoured enough food for hundreds of ordinary people and soon they had eaten everything that the land could provide. Next they turned to the sea and, striding into the water with their vast nets, pulled in thousands of fish at each throw. The coastal fish stocks declined and the local fishermen were ruined. Soon the people were starving and afraid. 'What can be done with these hungry men?' asked the people, and they prayed to the great god Pachacamac to help them.

One night, when the giants were sitting round their fires eating and drinking, the sky above them seemed to burst into flames and a sword of fire swept through them, destroying them completely. When the frightened Indians dared to approach the village next day, all they found were a few bones and skulls. The giants had gone forever.

When the Spaniards came, some claimed to have seen great bones and teeth and there is even a story that one bone had a Latin or old German inscription on it, proving, they said, that Europeans had been there before. Early this century archaeologists discovered the remains of stone-built wells in the area where the giants are supposed to have lived and there are also stone seats carved with birds, animals and images of long-forgotten deities. But no-one really knows whether the legend of the giants is based on an ancient invasion by strangers from a far-off land or whether it is just another story.

79

The walking idols

The people who lived in the Yungas, the fertile valleys which descend eastwards to the jungle from the Bolivian Altiplano, believed that long ago, before there were humans, idols and images walked about like men and women. They were known as huacas, a name which was later used for all kinds of holy objects.

These huacas had come from the coast to live in the foothills of the Andes but they did not become real mountain people. They were used to a sunny country with little rain; the only plants they knew were those they had grown themselves with the help of irrigation channels in the dry soil. In the more fertile mountain valleys, they admired the lush green plants and the animals they found grazing wild in the grasslands. But they were homesick—they longed for the sea with its teeming fish and for the dryness and warmth they knew.

One day a powerful new god named Huallallo arrived in the valley where the huacas were living and, guessing that they were foreigners and not living at their ease, he decided to make them his slaves. He cunningly arranged an ambush for them as they were trudging out to work in the fields and he killed or captured many of their men.

Huallallo's rule was harsh. He ordered that no couple should have more than two children and that of these, one was to be sacrificed to him. On the other hand, he brought great fertility to the land: seeds that were planted sprouted and ripened in five days and the valleys became the home of brilliantly coloured birds. So Huallallo kept the huacas in subjugation and gradually they lost their godlike powers and turned into ordinary human beings.

The great flood which is mentioned in so many of the myths of Central and South America, is supposed to have occurred during Huallallo's rule. An Indian, the descendant of one of the huacas, was pasturing his llamas near a mountain called Villcacoto when he noticed that one of the animals was looking miserable and was refusing to eat. He asked the llama what the matter was and the llama told him that in five days the sea would rush in from the coast to destroy the world.

'Master,' continued the llama, 'if you will take me and my fellow animals with you, we can find somewhere to shelter.'

So the man took enough food for five days and walked with his llamas to the very top of the mountain of Villcacoto. There they found thousands of other animals, all huddled together. There was no sign of any humans. The animals knew how to read the signs of nature but men, preoccupied with their own lives, felt nothing.

The flood came just as the llama had predicted, filling the valleys around and covering all the lower hilltops. Soon the shuddering animals were pressed even more tightly together, entirely surrounded by dark water. It came so close that the tip of the fox's tail dipped into it—and his tail has remained black ever since.

The people who had been huacas were washed away in the flood; only the man who listened to the llama was left alive and, they say, from him all the humans in the world descended.

The god Huallallo survived the flood but he, in turn, was defeated by a new, more powerful challenger. Pariacaca, a god of the mountain waters, defeated Huallallo in a contest of water and fire, driving the older deity into the forest forever and ruling the mountains in his place.

Nunguí's babies

A great variety of plants are grown as food in both the mountain and forest areas of South America. Staple crops vary with the different environments. Grains such as quinoa, and many varieties of potato, grow well in the cold climate of the Andes while manioc, yams and sweet potatoes flourish in the tropical rainforests. Maize, too, grows in many parts of the region.

When a tribe depends mainly on a single type of vegetable for its food, traditions and ceremonies grow up around it. The Jivaro Indians, for example, say that a goddess called Nunguí is responsible for helping manioc to push its way through the earth. She is hardly ever seen, but she is said to be about a metre tall, very fat, dressed in a plain black dress. Anyone who wants to grow healthy food plants must try to attract her to their plot of land and persuade her to stay there for as long as possible.

While she stays in the garden, Nunguí encourages the manioc to grow big and fat by dancing between the plants at night. In the day she disappears into the earth and the manioc loses its strength. That is why manioc must be dug out early in the morning, before its night-time goodness has vanished.

Before Nunguí will come, she must be provided with two things: first, a dancing song must be performed at nightfall so that she can dance to its rhythm; second, three pieces of jasper stone, known as Nunguí's babies, must be placed under an upturned food bowl in the garden.

The three stone babies are a reminder of the time before people knew about growing crops. In those days they ate different kinds of leaves and were often hungry. One day they went to a stream to try to catch some crabs and they saw there a little fat woman, all dressed in black, who was washing some roots in the water.
'Can you give us anything to eat?' asked the people.
'Take this baby and eat it,' said Nunguí, handing them a tuber of manioc. 'Whenever you want more, ask it to bring manioc, and the house will be full of good food.'

From that time on, the people grew manioc in their gardens and honoured its goddess Nunguí.

Another story, told by the Machiguenga tribe, who live on the eastern side of the Andes, explains how people learned to appreciate the different tastes of food. They say that once men had no teeth and ate rather like birds, without chewing. They knew nothing about cultivated plants and lived on lumps of potter's clay. It was the Moon who taught them to eat properly.

The Moon had married a young girl who bore him four sons and many daughters. He took three of his sons up into the sky with him. One son was very hot indeed and he was placed high up amongst the stars far, far away where he cannot be seen. Two other sons stayed with him and became the planet Venus and the Sun we see from the earth. The last son decided to live in the lower world as the Night Sun. We cannot see him, but he gives the stars their light. The daughters of the Moon stayed on earth and they became the cultivated plants—manioc, maize, banana and sweet potatoes.

In the early days, when people first discovered the plants, they used to treat them badly, cleaning them clumsily, scattering their skins or not bothering to cook them with the proper seasonings. When they came to eat, they simply gulped the food down, hardly knowing what they were tasting. Then the daughters would complain to the Moon: 'They give me nothing,' the Manioc daughter would weep. Or 'They throw nothing but pimiento into my pot. It's much too hot for me.'

But when they cooked the food well, or served it with meat and fish, the Manioc daughter would say, 'They are treating me well, father. They give me all I want.'

The daughters all complained to their father and gradually the people learned to listen to the Moon daughters, to savour their food, to value it for its taste as well as for its bulk. In return the Moon daughters grow contentedly in the gardens, and no-one goes hungry any more.

Spirits of the forest

To the south of the great Amazon River basin, the land rises to form a plateau of higher ground, cut by deep river valleys and stretching across south and east Brazil into northern Paraguay. The tribes who live there are very similar to the more northerly Amazonian Indians and once lived as hunters and gatherers, killing wild birds and animals for food and gathering fruits, roots and leaves. When white settlers arrived with their guns, game animals such as the peccary, on which the Indians depended for food, were overhunted and many Indians had to try to live by farming. Others were employed as labourers on the new settler-owned farms and ranches. Like other Indian tribes, their population has decreased rapidly since they have been in contact with white immigrants.

The first stories in this chapter come from the Karaja and Apinayé tribes, who live in the central and northern plateau area and speak dialects of a language called Ge. The other stories are from the Xingu tribes, a group of around fourteen tribes who live to the north of the highlands, around the Xingu river and its tributaries.

In 1961 a national park, covering some 8,500 square miles of forest land, was established in the Xingu tribal area. Tribes from outside the park are persuaded to live there only when conditions beyond its borders make it impossible for them to survive. Once there, contact with the European way of life is kept to a minimum: they are vaccinated against diseases and encouraged to live peacefully, but otherwise are left to live as they choose. Much of the credit for this goes to the three Villas Boas brothers, who mounted a campaign to convince Brazilians that the Indians were of most value to the community living in their own traditional way.

In spite of such efforts, the future of the Xingu tribes is threatened. Since the 1880s, their population has halved as people have been destroyed by western diseases, by exploitation as cheap labour and even by deliberate massacres. Some tribes now consist of no more than fifty individuals.

Today there is a new threat to the survivors as trunk roads are built across Xingu tribal lands, destroying hundreds of acres of forest and making it more and more difficult for the Indians who belong there to preserve their unique way of life.

The magic arrows

There were once two giant howler monkeys who spent all their time chasing and frightening the Indians in the forest. Several hunters tried to catch them, but without success. Then one day two brothers from the Karaja tribe decided to try their luck.

On their way to the howler monkeys' lair they met a toad woman.
'I'll tell you how to catch the monkeys,' she croaked, 'but on one condition. One of you must promise to marry me.'

The brothers looked at the toad woman disdainfully. 'Marry an ugly thing like you?' they said. 'We'll manage without your help, thank you.'

The toad woman sighed and hopped back to her home and the brothers strode into the forest, laughing at her disappointment.

Before long they saw the howler monkeys speeding towards them through the branches, each carrying a heavy throwing stick. The monkeys looked fierce and powerful and moved so swiftly through the trees that the brothers had no time to aim their own arrows before the monkeys were on them. Terrified, they fled out of the jungle and were never seen again.

Now the two hunters had a young brother, a sickly young man whose body was covered in sores and ulcers. While the brothers were fleeing from the forest, he was wandering at the edge of the village, shooting at birds. As usual, he missed his target and as usual he lost his arrow in the undergrowth. He was searching for it rather half-heartedly when a quiet voice said, 'Can I help you?'

Looking down, the young man saw a snake peering from its hole in the ground.
'Is this your arrow?' it asked. 'It has fallen into my house.'

The young man thanked the snake and, since he had nothing else to do, he stayed to talk for a while.
'What is the matter with your skin?' asked the snake. 'It looks very painful. What medicine are you using?'
'No-one can cure me,' said the young man. 'Only my grandmother will look after me—and I'm no good for anything. I can't even hunt. I always lose my arrows.'

The snake felt sorry for the young man. 'I have some ointment that will help you,' he said.

The young man stayed with the snake for several days and every morning and evening he smeared ointment on his face and body. Before long, his skin was as smooth as a child's. Overjoyed, he thanked the snake once more. 'Now I must go and find my brothers,' he said and explained how they had set out to kill the howler monkeys but had not returned.
'Those are no ordinary monkeys,' said the snake, 'but demons in disguise. Your brothers will not catch them. But you can—with the help of this magic arrow.' He gave the young man a long, pointed arrow, then added: 'On the way you will meet a toad woman and she will ask you to marry her. Don't be alarmed. Agree to do as she asks—she will help you then and you'll find that being married to a toad is not as strange as you expect. Oh and one more thing. Aim the arrow at the monkeys. It will hit them both at the same time and as they fall, the demons will vanish into the air forever.'

Everything happened just as the snake had said. The young man met the toad woman and was polite and kind to her. In return she showed him where to hide and wait for the monkeys and when they arrived, she helped him to aim correctly. As soon as the arrow struck home, the demons left in a swirl of smoke and the monkeys' empty skins fell to the ground with the arrow still in place.

The young man carried the trophies back to the snake and the snake gave him a whole armful of magic arrows in return.
'Now you will never lose an arrow again,' said the snake.

The young man returned to his village with the toad and made his way to his grandmother's hut, very anxious about what she might say. As soon as he led the toad inside, however, she changed into a beautiful young girl who turned to greet him with a smile. From that day on, the young man's life was transformed. With the help of his magic arrows he became a famous hunter and he and his wife lived together healthily and happily for the rest of their lives.

The origin of fire

There was once a man who, while out hunting with his young brother, saw a macaw's nest high up on a steep cliff face. It had two small macaws in it and since macaw feathers are valuable, he thought he would like to catch the birds to rear at home for sale.

The cliff in which the macaw had nested was, however, very high and so smooth and straight that it was impossible to climb. The man looked around to see what he could use as a ladder. Young saplings were growing all around and he quickly chopped one down and lopped off its branches to make a kind of ladder tree. Leaning it against the cliff, he told his brother to climb up to the nest.

The boy scrambled up and clambered from the ladder tree to the ledge on which the nest was built. As he reached out for the young birds, the parents attacked him angrily, rushing at him, pecking and flapping their wings, screaming loudly. The boy was frightened and looked timidly down to his brother far below.

'I can't do it,' he shouted tearfully. 'I want to come down.'

But the brother, angry at the boy's feebleness, knocked the ladder tree crossly away and strode off into the forest.

The small boy did not know what to do. He sat there, clinging to the rock, unable to move, for what seemed like a very long time. Night came and the boy slept fitfully. At dawn the sunlight came filtering softly through the canopy of trees and still there was no sign of his brother. By now the boy was very hungry and thirsty, and lonely, too. The parent macaws flew off one at a time for food, flapping their wings in his face as they landed and took off. The young birds jeered at him from the safety of the nest. Another night came and another day dawned. When the sun was high overhead, the boy plucked up courage to explore the cliff and, gripping with his hands and feet like a monkey, he sidled along the ledge. Far below, on the forest floor, a passing jaguar saw the shadow moving on the ground. Deceived for a moment by the flickering sunlight, he pounced on the dancing shadow, grabbing with his claws at

nothing. In spite of his hunger, the little boy laughed and the jaguar looked up in annoyance. 'What are you doing up there?' he asked.

'I've been up here for days,' complained the boy. 'I climbed up that ladder tree but I was dizzy and my brother was angry with me and he left me to the bad-tempered birds up here. Mind you, I was trying to steal the two chicks, so they have a right to suspect me.'

'Two young macaws, eh,' said the jaguar, licking his lips. 'Why, what a nice . . . I mean how interesting. Would you let me have a look at them?'

Desperation made the boy brave and now he plunged his hand into the nest and plucked out the two chicks, ignoring the frantic pecks of the parent birds. He threw down first one, then the other (he felt they deserved this anyway for making him suffer so much) and the jaguar gobbled them up greedily.

'If I bring you the ladder tree, will you come down too?' asked the jaguar.

Seeing what had happened to the macaws, the boy said he would rather not.

'It's all right,' said the jaguar. 'I wouldn't dream of eating you. You must be thirsty up there. I'll find you some water if you like.'

The jaguar helpfully replaced the ladder tree and the boy climbed shakily down. Good as his word, the jaguar carried the boy on his back to a small creek and waited while the boy drank as much of the clear water as he wanted. Then, like an exhausted puppy, the boy fell fast asleep. The jaguar lay down to keep watch and when it began to grow dark, pinched his arm gently to wake him up. Then he washed him carefully with water from the creek and told him that, as he had no children of his own, he would be the boy's father and take care of him. The boy scrambled on the jaguar's back once more and was carried off to his house.

As soon as he was inside the house, the boy noticed a great jatoba tree trunk lying on the floor, smouldering at one end. In those days the Indians had no fire and the boy was most intrigued.

'What's that smoking on the floor?' he asked. 'That's fire,' said the jaguar. 'Here, see what it can do.' And he handed the boy a piece of roasted meat. After the sun-dried meat the boy was used to, it tasted most excellent. 'And that's not all,' said the jaguar. 'Wait until it is night.'

When it was quite dark the boy and the jaguar huddled round the fire and the boy felt its comforting warmth and saw the light from its flames. He dozed happily, waking about midnight for another snack of roast meat, then falling deeply asleep again.

The next morning, before daybreak, the jaguar went hunting and when the boy awoke some time later, only the jaguar's wife was there. She was not very friendly and when the boy asked for some food, she bared her teeth in an unpleasant way and gave him nothing. The boy ran out to find the jaguar and told him what had happened. When they came back to the house the jaguar scolded his wife but she laughed it off, saying she had just been joking; it all meant nothing. However, the same thing happened the next day and the day after that, so that when the jaguar gave the boy a bow and arrows and told him to practise shooting at termite nests, it was not surprising that he made the jaguar's wife his first target, instead.

The boy was rather frightened by what he had done and worried about the jaguar's reaction. To his surprise, the jaguar simply said, 'Oh well, never mind,' but then he added, 'all the same, it might be an idea if you went back to your village now. Here's the way you have to go . . .' He explained the route carefully, telling him to follow the line of the creek. 'But please be careful. If a rock or an aroeira tree calls out to you, you can answer back; but if a rotten dead tree calls out, don't say a word. Just keep very quiet.'

The jaguar gave the boy some roast meat for his journey and the boy set out. He had not gone very far when he heard a gruff voice calling out to him, asking where he was going. Looking round, the only thing he saw was a smooth grey boulder in the stream. He answered politely and went on his way. Some time later he heard another voice asking him where he was going. This time the voice whispered and rustled and he knew that it came from an aroeira tree that grew on the creek banks. Again he answered politely and went on his way. On and on he walked, growing tired and hot as the day wore on.

'Where are you going?' said an old, hoarse voice

suddenly in his ear, making him jump. 'I'm going home to my village,' said the boy without thinking. 'I wish I was there now.'

Then he remembered the jaguar's words. There beside him was the rotting stump of an old forest tree, covered in creepers and mosses. The boy covered his mouth with his hand and looked fearfully all around. Everything was quiet and still.

'The jaguar was just trying to frighten me,' he decided, but deep inside he sensed that something had changed. Although he did not know it, the jaguar had given him good advice. If he had answered only the rock and the aroeira tree, he and all his people would have lived as long as the rocks and the forest trees. By answering the rotten stump, he had condemned his people to a human life span so that they grew old and died within about fifty years.

The boy was still some distance from his village and his adventures were not yet over. A few miles further on he heard a fourth voice and again he replied. This time to his surprise he saw a figure that looked just like his father but when he ran to greet him, the figure grabbed him and, after a fierce struggle, bundled him inside a large carrying basket. It was not his father at all, but an ogre, the magalon kamduré, who lived on the flesh of animals and men. The ogre stalked slowly through the forest, on the lookout for more animals to take home to his family. Soon he put the basket down so that he could hunt more effectively.

'If you intend to catch a lot of game, why don't you make a trail through the forest first,' said the boy from inside the basket. 'It will be difficult to make your way with so much meat on your shoulders.'

The ogre, who though strong and powerful was not very intelligent, thought this a good idea and he strode off into the forest, swinging at the undergrowth on either side with his stick. As soon as he was out of sight, the boy pushed up the lid of the basket and clambered out. He placed a heavy stone in the bottom so that the ogre would not notice how light the basket had become and was just about to run off when he heard the ogre returning. Crouching in the bushes he watched the ogre place his new catch in the basket, swing it

onto his shoulders, and stride off into the forest. Without waiting a moment longer, the boy ran off as fast as he could and did not stop until he had reached his own village.

At last he was home and, as his family sat round, he told them everything that had happened. Of all the strange things he related, the Indians found the idea of fire the most interesting and before the evening was over, they had decided that they, too, must see the strange flame that gave heat and cooked meat. Together they made their way to the jaguar's home and listened as he explained the nature of fire.

'Here,' he said, holding out a thick, smouldering log to the boy's father. 'I have adopted your son and love him like my own child. Since it is not suitable for him to live with me and share my fire, take this with you for your own house. Cook your meat with it and warm yourselves by it in the night. Look after it well and it will be your servant.'

From that time on the Indians knew fire.

The sleep tree

A hunter called Uaicá was walking in the forest one day when he came upon a crowd of animals all fast asleep under a large tree. He went up to investigate and as he stood under the deep shade of the branches he suddenly began to feel dizzy. Staggering and stumbling, he fell down among the animals and was immediately fast asleep.

As he slept he dreamed vividly of strange animals and of people he did not know. He also dreamed of his own tribe, the Jurana, and in his dream he talked to one of his ancestors, Sinaá, who told him many secret things.

At sunset he woke and hurried home but next day he returned, strangely fascinated by the new world he had glimpsed. Again he felt dizzy and again he fell asleep and entered the world of his ancestors. For several days Uaicá did nothing but sleep under the tree, eating nothing from sunrise to sunset. The dreams were so real that he could think of nothing else. Finally, Sinaá, his ancestor, told him: 'This must be your last visit to the tree, Uaicá. If you come here again you will be in danger. You have seen more than enough of my world.'

When Uaicá woke up he stared sadly at the tree, knowing that he would not see it again. However, he scraped some bark from it before he left and on the way home went down to the river's edge and mixed the bark with water to make a strange, bitter drink. The effect of the drink was startling for he immediately began to behave like someone possessed, dancing and leaping until he jumped right into the river and began to catch fish with his bare hands. At last the intoxicating effect wore off and Uaicá made his way back to the village, carrying his armfuls of fish and feeling strangely elated.

Uaicá did not go back to the tree in the forest but he continued to make infusions from its bark and by the time he had finished his supply, he had many of the tree's magic powers. One day when the village shaman or holy man had failed to cure a sick child, its parents brought it to Uaicá and he was able to make it well again.

More and more people brought him their illnesses and everyone he touched was healed. His powers seemed to grow greater and soon he found himself dreaming again, talking to Sinaá and learning about the spirit world. His fame spread through the forest.

All went well with Uaicá until he married a quarrelsome wife. For her, nothing was right and one day, after a particularly tiresome exchange, Uaicá's mother took a stick and chased her out of the village. The wife's relations were very angry at this treatment and they plotted together to kill Uaicá in revenge. They waited until Uaicá came home with his evening catch of fish and, when he sat down to eat, his brother-in-law crept up behind him with a great cudgel, intending to bring it down on his head. But it is not so easy to outwit a shaman! Uaicá could see all round him without looking and as the cudgel came swinging down, he ducked out from under it and vanished. To their astonishment his wife's relations found themselves standing on a bare patch of earth: Uaicá had taken his house, his garden and all his belongings with him, there was no trace of any of them to be seen.

The village people searched for Uaicá for many days and at last his brother-in-law found him some miles away, clearing a new garden in a patch of forest. Uaicá behaved as if nothing unusual had happened and he allowed himself to be persuaded to return. For a time life returned to normal, but then the evil brother-in-law tried to kill him a second time, stealing up behind him as he sat on a rock eating his evening meal. Again Uaicá saw what was happening without even looking round. This time he spoke before he vanished.

'I shall never come back to the village,' he said sadly. 'And you will never know the things I have learned from our ancestor Sinaá. You have forfeited your right to know the secrets of the other world.'

With that he disappeared into the rock on which he was sitting and was never seen again. They say that Uaicá still lives inside the rock, dreaming and talking to Sinaá from one year to the next. If anyone touches the rock, he will die. One day a man of the Jurana tribe went right up to the rock and saw Uaicá's hand reaching out of a crack, inviting him in to the spirit world. But though the man looked for the door he could not find it and he turned away, trembling.

The language of birds

A man who had quarrelled with his wife once went off into the forest to smoke in peace and quiet. He rolled two cigars and sat down with his back against the thick trunk of a tall tree.
'I'd like to be you, Tree,' he said.
'No you wouldn't,' said the tree. 'It is very difficult being a tree. For one thing you can never sleep at all, for if you do, you simply die.'

The man finished his first cigar, then moved off to smoke the second in a different place. This time he came to a smaller tree, with supple branches and twigs.
'I'd like to be you,' he said to it.
'No you wouldn't,' replied the tree. 'People are always coming up and lopping off small branches for bows. Trees like me live a very short time.'

The young man wandered on into the forest, thinking how difficult life was, when he saw a column of smoke ahead of him. Drawing nearer, he saw a group of bird people burning the grass in a clearing.
'Hello,' said the birds. 'What are you doing?'
'Nothing special,' said the man. 'May I watch?'

The bird people invited the man to sit down and smoke with them. 'Why don't you come to see our village?' they asked. 'We are clearing the forest to make a new garden.'

The birds invited the man because they knew he came from the same village as a man they feared and hated, named Avatsiu. Avatsiu was always hunting and killing the birds and they hoped the young man would help them to destroy him. In their village they made him very much at home and next day, when he felt quite settled in, they decided to make him look more like one of them. The bird people mixed some glue and covered the young man with bright feathers, complete with wings and a long tail. He looked quite a handsome bird but when he shook his feathers a few times to see if they were firmly fixed, one fell out.

The birds whispered to one another that this was a bad omen but still they pursued their plan. First they took him to the place where they trained their young and showed him how to fly up to the top of a tree and pick a termite from its bark. The man managed to fly clumsily up but he completely failed to find the termite. Then they showed him how to pick up a stone and hover with it in the air. The man swooped down but missed the stone and landed heavily on his head. He tried several times but the result was always the same, and eventually he gave up and returned to the bird village.

In spite of the young man's failures, the birds decided to take him with them when they went to attack Avatsiu. Next morning they flew all together in a large flock and perched in a tree in front of Avatsiu's house.
'Now, wait for us and don't be impatient,' said the birds, for they could see that the young man considered himself a rather fine bird. Their good advice was wasted. As soon as Avatsiu came out to see what all the noise was about, the young man, eager to show off his skills, swooped down from the branch and tried to grasp Avatsiu in his feet. Once again he missed the target and Avatsiu caught him deftly by the neck and popped him straight into a pot of boiling water, feathers and all.

The birds were very sad to lose their young bird-man and they flew away at once to discuss the next move.
'Perhaps he has a son,' suggested one. 'He might help us avenge the bird-man's death.'
'I know he has a son,' said a small red bird called

the Ararauna. 'I have often seen him playing.'

The small red bird was sent to fetch the son and was soon perched on a tree near the family hut. The man's wife was preparing food in front of the hut and she called her son to see the strange bird. The boy ran into the house to fetch his bow and arrows but when he crept up to the tree, the Ararauna, who had been watching carefully out of the corner of his eye, fluttered on to another bush, then to another and another until they were out of sight of the house.

Then, to the boy's surprise, the bird spoke to him. 'Put your bow and arrow away,' it said. 'We want you to help us kill Avatsiu and avenge your father's death.'

The little boy knew how his father had died and he was very pleased to help. 'But first I must tell my mother where I am going,' he said.

Of course his mother was very worried when she heard what he was going to do. 'Your father was killed trying to behave like one of the bird people,' she said. 'Am I to lose my son as well?' However, the boy insisted and in the end she allowed him to go.

'But listen carefully. Never attack Avatsiu from in front. Creep up from behind and kill him by stealth. It is the only way.'

'Don't worry,' said the boy. 'I shall be all right. And I'll bring you some feathers back, too. Give me some mats to carry them in.'

The boy returned confidently to where the Ararauna was waiting and was led through the forest to the bird village. The birds came out to greet him one by one.

'Now my son,' said the chief bird gravely. 'We will help you to avenge your father's death. You must kill Avatsiu.'

'I agree,' said the boy, 'but how? If we grab him from the front he will kill us as he killed my father and so many of your people. We must creep up on him from behind and take him by surprise.'

'This boy certainly knows what he is doing,' murmured the birds.

Next morning they took glue and feathers and covered the boy completely with feathers. When they asked him to shake his new wings every feather remained firmly fixed in place. At the training tree he flew up immediately and neatly picked the termite from the bark as if he had been doing it all his life. Then he swooped down, picked up a large stone and hovered high in the air with it.

'This time we shall succeed,' said the birds to one another, and without waiting any longer they all flew off to perch in the tree in front of Avatsiu's house.

'I'm going round the back,' said the boy and he flew silently round the hut, leading the other birds to a carefully chosen spot on the roof. When Avatsiu came out, the boy swooped down and, seizing him in his talons, just managed to lift him off the ground. Immediately three great eagles flew down to help him and together they raised him higher and higher until the village below looked like a child's toy. Then the birds and the bird-boy released their hold and Avatsiu, who had killed so many of them, plunged down to his death.

The birds gathered round his body to make sure he was really dead and the chief bird made a proclamation.

'This man Avatsiu brought death to our people but from his blood we shall receive a valuable gift. Until today we have had no language of our own, but have used the language of humans. From now on we shall each have a language appropriate to our own kind, a language which will express our thoughts to one another in our own way.'

One by one the birds came forward to receive their languages. The first to speak were the eagles then the hummingbird and the horned screamer, the dove and the curassow, the parrot and the macaw, the woodpecker and the little red Ararauna bird. At first their voices did not all seem suitable for the hummingbird had a deep, hoarse language and the horned screamer a shrill squeak. These two decided to exchange and others followed their example until each bird had its own way of speaking. The ceremony of language lasted all night long and as dawn came, they all began to sing at once, each trying to out-sing the others in a wave of joyful sound.

As the sun rose they turned to thank the boy who had helped them and, plucking their best feathers, they filled the mats he had brought until he could carry no more. Loaded with their brilliant plumage and surrounded by their music, he returned triumphantly to his home.

Tales from the Amazon

The Amazon basin with its great network of rivers extends for many thousands of square miles through northern Brazil. The rivers are fed from two main sources: water flowing from the Andes and the very heavy rainfall which pours down over the jungle. Although vast areas are being destroyed to make way for commercial plantations, the Amazon forest is still the largest area of rainforest in the world and contains thousands of different species of plants and animals. Great hardwood trees grow with tall, straight trunks, branching out into a thick canopy of leaves high above the forest floor. Creepers and vines cover the ground and festoon the branches. Birds, animals and insects of all kinds live at every level of the forest and in the wide, slow-flowing rivers are giant snakes, turtles, alligators and an abundance of fish.

The Indians who occupy this apparently dangerous and hostile world live mainly along the smaller rivers that feed the Amazon, using the waterways as their main communication routes. Perfectly in tune with the natural world around them, they use the resources of the forest and rivers for all their needs. They shoot and trap animals and fish and they know the uses of the wild fruits and plants. Living in family groups, they clear areas of forest by cutting down and burning the smaller trees so that they can grow food crops. But the soil is usually thin and poor and when it is exhausted they must move on to clear a new garden elsewhere.

As the forest is so dense, tribes become isolated from one another and it is not always easy for one group to understand another. Their history has been very bloodthirsty and cruelty in war is often reflected in their legends, which are full of forest strangers, giants and men who live underground. Their gods are the spirits and demons of the forest. All over the world the snake is considered as a supernatural being and, whether it stands for wisdom or evil, has always held pride of place among the animals. To the Amazonian Indians, Big Cobra, who appears in the story 'How night came' is one of the chief animal symbols of power.

Today the forest Indians and their way of life are more at risk than ever before and, although there may still be tribes living in the traditional way deep in the forest, sadly, their numbers grow smaller every day as they are overwhelmed by an alien European culture.

How night came

Once, long ago at the beginning of all time, there was no such thing as night. The Indians tell that it was always day and that night slept at the bottom of the waters, extending like a long, dark shadow along the bed of the river, watched over by Big Cobra. In those days there were people but no animals and all things had the gift of speech: trees, flowers, rocks, rivers—everything that today is silent, could in those days talk freely. As it was always daytime, no-one slept.

One day, in those far-off times, the daughter of Big Cobra married a young and handsome man. The young man had three very faithful servants who were always at his side and up to the time of his marriage he never found any fault with them. After he was married, however, he began to grumble at them. 'Don't stay near me all the time! Go for a walk out of my sight. I want to sleep.' He turned to his wife. 'Leave me alone for a while. I want to sleep.'

'We can't sleep,' replied his wife. 'It is not night time.'

'I don't care,' replied the husband. 'I want to sleep now.'

'I tell you it's impossible,' said the wife. 'We have no night here.'

'What is night, anyway? There's no such thing,' said the husband crossly.

'Of course there is,' replied the wife. 'My father has it. He never lets it leave him. Now you go to sleep if you can, it is just too light for me. If you want me to sleep too, go and find the night—it's with my father at the bottom of the river.'

The man called his servants back and asked his wife to explain exactly how they should proceed.

'Go to my father's house,' she explained, 'and do exactly what he says. But be careful, be very, very careful to obey him in everything.'

'My servants are not children,' answered the husband angrily. 'They don't have to be told twice what to do.'

The three servants took a canoe from the river bank and paddled upstream until they arrived at a place where their river joined a much wider, slowly flowing waterway. There they clambered up the bank and started to splash about on the shore line, playing with small stones and throwing them into the deep water. Far below at the bottom of the river, Big Cobra felt the disturbance and swam up to see what was happening.

'Oh it's you,' he grumbled when he saw the three servants. 'I know why you are here—my daughter has sent you.'

The three servants nodded, dumb with surprise. Big Cobra dived down to the bottom of the river again and a few minutes later reappeared with a Tucuma coconut which he gave to them. A crack in its shell showed that it had been opened but it had been completely resealed with a kind of resin.

'Whatever you do, don't open this coconut,' said Big Cobra, 'for if it is opened, the things it contains will be lost and you will be lost with them.'

The three servants took the coconut, clambered back into their canoe and set off for home. They had not gone very far, however, when they heard a little noise coming from inside the coconut:

'Ten ten ten, shee shee shee, croa croa croa, cree cree cree . . .'

These are the sounds that toads and frogs make, croaking and singing at night time but as the three servants did not know what night was, they did not recognize its sounds. Instead they began to discuss what to do.

'Let's open the coconut and see what's inside,' said the youngest.

'No,' said the second, 'for if we do, all the things inside will be lost and we shall be lost with them. You heard what Big Cobra said. Come on, let's get home.'

They paddled on down the river but the more they paddled, the more their oars seemed to whisper 'Open it, open it.' The third servant, who had so far not given his opinion, paddled absent-mindedly, his whole attention on the coconut which continued to sing and croak 'Cree cree cree, ten ten ten, shee shee shee . . .'

'Let's just take a peep,' he said at last. 'We don't need to take off all the resin, only a little bit so we can look inside.'

Still the second servant said no. 'I'm as curious as you are to see what's inside,' he told them, 'but we promised the girl not to disobey Big Cobra.'

'As for that,' said the first servant, 'we heard what Big Cobra said but we didn't actually promise anything to him.'

'What have we to do with them anyway, that father and that daughter?' added the third servant. 'We are servants of the husband. not the wife.'

In the end the three servants stowed their paddles safely in the boat, sat together in the middle and lit a small fire. With this they managed to melt the resin that sealed the coconut. The resin melted all at once and splashed painfully onto their faces and arms; and instead of opening just a little way, the coconut split right in two. At that moment, everything went completely dark.

'Now we really are lost,' cried the third servant. 'Big Cobra will know that we opened the Tucuma coconut.'

'Couldn't we say that it fell on the ground and cracked open by itself?' asked the first servant.

'It doesn't help to tell lies,' said the second servant. 'They will know perfectly well that we opened it through curiosity.'

Very frightened, the three servants paddled on into the darkness towards their home.

When the servants released the night from the coconut, darkness had fallen over the whole country, including, of course, the home of Big Cobra's daughter and her husband. She did not seem alarmed.

'Ah, so they have let loose the night,' she said. 'But don't worry, it just means we have to sit and wait for the morning when it will be light again.'

'Oh no,' said her husband. 'It means we can sleep.' Together, Big Cobra's daughter and her husband lay down on the grass bed in the corner of their hut.

The night that had escaped from the coconut was a magical night. As the young couple lay in one another's arms, the night transformed all the lifeless things in the forest outside into something new. Pebbles turned into toads and insects, dried, dead trees and fallen leaves became animals. A wicker basket standing outside the hut became a jaguar. Every piece of debris floating in the river became a fish or water bird. A fisherman sleeping in his canoe became a pelican. A tree trunk floating on the river current became a Pirarucu fish. A bunch of dried reeds became a turtle. The young couple's lives were also changed that night,

for nine months later a son was born to them.

Before they fell asleep, Big Cobra's daughter and her husband lay contemplating the darkness all around them.

'Why did your father keep night to himself at the bottom of the river?' asked the young man.

'He was afraid that things would get lost,' said his wife sleepily. 'Wait until tomorrow, then we will see if everything appears in its place again.'

When the dawn star rose in the dark sky, Big Cobra's daughter rose and went to the door of the hut.

'Come,' she said, 'dawn is near. I am going to divide the night from the day so that everything will know when one is ending and the other beginning.'

Taking a strand of her hair, she wound it into a curl around her finger and said: 'You shall be a Cujubi bird.' At once the hair turned into a small bird, perching on her finger. Then Big Cobra's daughter painted the bird's feathers white with a dye made from clay called tabatinga and its legs scarlet with a vermilion dye made from urucum. 'Cujubi bird, you shall always sing at sunrise,' she said.

The bird flew off singing into the pale light, and she chose another strand of hair and curled it around her finger. This time she put a pinch of ash on the curl and said, 'You shall be called Inhambu bird and you shall sing both at nightfall and at dawn.' At once a second bird appeared on her finger, paused for a moment to try its wings, then flew off singing into the pale light.

In this way Big Cobra's daughter created one by one all the birds of the forest. Each time she rolled up a strand of hair into a curl and called out a name, a new bird appeared. She painted the birds with different dyes so that they would be distinct from one another: she painted one parrot green with a yellow head, another with a touch of scarlet, another with a patch of white or yellow. She painted one macaw bright blue, another blue and scarlet. One toucan she painted black with a yellow crop, another black and scarlet. She painted the birds in a thousand colours to brighten up the dark forest. Before each flew from her finger, she gave it its own song and from that day on, the birds all sang at their appointed time: some during the night, some in the day, all

together at the first breaking of dawn to make the day happy when it appeared, in the hope each time that perhaps it would stay on earth forever.

The young husband and wife were still standing outside their hut listening to the new sounds of the birds and looking with new eyes at all the familiar things which had disappeared from view in the night when the three servants appeared shamefacedly before them. The husband stared at them angrily. 'You failed me,' he said gravely, 'for you disobeyed Big Cobra and opened the coconut of Tucuma and let loose the night which was imprisoned inside it. The world we know was lost in the darkness and so shall you be. You shall be monkeys, spending your lives jumping from tree to tree in search of food and always frightened of the night.' As the young man turned away, three monkeys fled from him into the forest.

It is said that the monkeys' black mouths and the yellow marks which they bear to this day on their arms came from the resin of the coconut which scarred them as it melted. When night falls, these monkeys start to howl, telling the world that in the darkness everyone, including the monkeys themselves, will be lost.

Perhaps, however, even the monkeys know that things may not be as bad as they fear. The new dawn will break; Inhambu and Cujubi will sing and the new day will awaken happily. The three monkeys, from one hour to the next, from darkness to light, will become ordinary human beings once again.

The two parrots

The Sun was out hunting one day when he met a boy with two very young parrots. The birds were so small that they could hardly fly and Sun liked them so much that he took them from the boy and carried them home with the idea of bringing them up himself as pets. He chose the one with the brightest plumage for himself and gave the other to his companion, the Moon who, like the Sun, was in the form of a young man.

The two friends fed and cared for the parrots well and they became very tame. Every day Sun and Moon would spend hours with the birds, allowing them to perch on their fingers, stroking their bright feathers and teaching them how to talk like human beings. One day one parrot said to the other: 'I am really sick with worry at our masters' way of life; they come back tired out every evening from hunting and before they can rest they have to prepare supper for themselves. Let's help them if we can.'

The second parrot agreed and in an instant both had turned into girls. Immediately they started to make an evening meal for Sun and Moon, one preparing and cooking the food, the other standing guard at the door so that if either of the men returned they would have time to turn back into parrots again.

At dusk Sun and Moon walked home from hunting as usual. While they were still quite a distance away they heard a regular thudding noise coming from the direction of their hut, 'Pum, pum, pum'.
'Listen,' said Sun. 'Some enormous animal is striding through the forest towards us. Let's hurry home before he finds us.' The two men quickened their pace but as they drew nearer to their hut, the noise increased, making the ground shake under their feet with its insistent beat, pum, pum, pum.
'That's not an animal,' said Moon. 'It sounds more like the pounding of a huge pestle crushing corn. Whoever is doing it must be immensely strong—and he seems to be in a hurry too.'
'That's true,' said Sun. 'But can't you hear, the noise is coming from our hut. Let's see who is inside.'

They ran towards the hut and were only a few steps from the door when the noise stopped abruptly. They entered cautiously: there was no-one to be seen but on the floor before the fire were two bowls of maize meal, steaming hot and obviously freshly made. Looking at one another in amazement, Sun and Moon searched the hut. They looked in the large pots of stored grain to see if anyone was hiding there. They turned the baskets of vegetables upside down. They moved the piles of animal skins; they even sifted through the ashes of the fire to see if they could find a clue but there was no sign of anyone.

Perched as usual on their wooden pole, their

eager eyes full of pleasure, the two parrots stuck out their necks and cried, 'Cra, cra, cra.'
'There's no-one here but the parrots,' said the Moon at last. 'And they could not have done it.'
'Of course not, they wouldn't know how to,' said Sun. 'And even if they knew, they couldn't do it because they have no hands. But look, Moon, someone *has* been here.' He pointed to human footprints on the earth floor, footprints crossing and recrossing the floor in front of the fire but never passing through the door. They examined the ground outside the hut carefully but could find no signs there at all.

The next day Sun and Moon were once more hunting in the forest. Once more they heard the same strange noise, like the thudding of corn being pounded on a hard floor. Once more they searched every corner of the hut and once more found nothing but the two parrots looking innocently on and the marks of footprints on the beaten earth floor, inside but never outside the hut. Every day after that was the same: their meal was ready for them when they returned, the two parrots were preening themselves on their pole and footprints criss-crossed the earth floor.

As time went on, Sun became more and more intrigued by the mystery. One day he said to Moon: 'Today let's pretend we are going out hunting as usual. But instead of going to the forest, we'll hide just outside, one on either side of the hut. As soon as we hear the pounding of the pestle as it crushes the corn, we'll run into the hut. You take the back door, I'll take the front.'

Moon approved of the plan and next day they put it into effect; they took their bows and arrows, prepared themselves for the hunt, said good-bye to their parrots and set off purposefully towards the forest. Before they reached the forest edge, they turned and crept stealthily back to take up their positions in front of and behind the hut, where two clumps of trees hid them from sight.

At first all they could hear was the contented chattering of the parrots but very soon they began to hear girls' voices and laughter coming from inside the hut. Then, sure enough, they heard the now familiar thudding sound of corn being pounded. At once Sun and Moon leaped from their hiding places and rushed into the hut, Sun racing through the front door, Moon through the

back. The two girls saw that they had no time to change back into parrots so they calmly sat down and bowed their heads politely.

Both Sun and Moon stood still in the doorways, gazing at the two girls, who were far more beautiful than any they had seen before. Although they were very alike, the girls' hair was strikingly different: one had shining golden hair, the other jet black. Both wore it long, hanging loose right down to their waists. Moon took a step forward and was just about to speak to them when Sun stopped him with a movement of his hand. He wanted to be the first to speak.
'So it was you who has been preparing our meals every day,' he said, addressing the girl who seemed to him to be the more beautiful of the two. 'Where have you come from?'
'We felt sorry for you coming back every evening exhausted from hunting and then having to make your meal before you could rest your tired bodies. But don't you know us? We are your parrots. We have transformed ourselves into humans to cook your food. But now . . .'
'Now you stay as you are,' shouted Sun, shining with pleasure so that the whole hut was filled with light.

Without looking up, the girl said quietly, 'Then you must decide which of us each of you wants to marry.'

Sun cried without even pausing to think, 'I want to marry you.'

The girl who had been a parrot smiled. 'Well, that's the second time you've chosen me, then,' she said, for she was the parrot that Sun had chosen to keep for himself at the beginning.
'And I want to marry you,' cried Moon to the black-haired girl. 'For you are more beautiful than the night sky itself with its million stars.'

So Sun married the golden-haired parrot girl and Moon took the black-haired parrot girl as his wife. For a time they all lived very happily together, four people in the same hut. However, it was not a very big hut and they soon decided to take turns in sleeping there. Sun and his wife slept there at night while Moon and his wife slept there during the day. It is for that reason that Moon never sleeps now by night but wanders about until dawn when Sun goes out to hunt, carrying his bows and arrows as he stalks across the world.

The origin of bark masks

The Tucuna people of the north-west Amazon forests use masks made of bark cloth in funeral rites and other religious ceremonies. This story explains why.

There was once a cave in the forest where many demons lived. They raided all the villages around, stealing stocks of smoked meat and harassing the villagers. One day a party of travellers passed by and noticed mysterious tracks leading from one of the villages right up to the cave entrance.
'It looks as if someone has been dragging heavy bundles along there,' said the leader, 'but the villagers seem to be all away hunting, so we cannot ask them. How strange.'

As they stood staring at the cave the demons appeared at the entrance trying to lure them in with smiles and beckoning gestures. The leader turned away and the group made their camp at a safe distance.

Among the travellers was a woman who was about to have a child and they decided to stay there until she was safely delivered. Unfortunately, they had run very short of food. They did not like to hunt in another tribe's territory and there was no-one in the village with whom they could barter for a meal. Just as they were wondering what to do, a giant paca came wandering into their camp. In a moment it had been caught and killed and it provided them all with an evening meal.

The next day the men went off to find more food, leaving the woman behind. While they were away, her baby was born and she was holding it in her arms for the first time when suddenly a small, furry demon appeared.
'Don't be afraid,' it said. 'I am a friend. 'I've come to warn you because I don't want you and your baby to be hurt. Last night when you ate that paca you did a terrible thing. The paca was no ordinary animal but was one of us, a demon. In fact he was my own son. Tonight we shall take our revenge.'
'But I did not even eat any of the paca meat,' said the woman. 'I was not hungry.'
'In that case you of all people must be saved,' continued the furry demon earnestly. 'The only way you can escape is by climbing that tree.' He

pointed to a particularly tall tree nearby. 'As you climb, strip off the bark behind you so that the demons will not be able to follow you. Remember to do as I say. I shall not be able to help you tonight.'

The travellers soon returned with food they had managed to obtain in another village and the woman told them what had happened. They were so pleased with their day's work and with the fact that there was now a new member of the tribe that they did not really listen to what she was saying.

The meal was cooked on the camp fire and the party settled down to eat, but the woman could not forget what had happened and even as they were eating she seemed to hear the howls and hunting calls of the demons.
'Can't you hear them?' she cried, hugging her baby.
'Why, that's just the noise of the wind in the trees. Come, eat more food,' said the others.

Soon they had all eaten so much that they fell asleep around the fire, snoring like jaguars. Only the woman stayed awake, watching.

Then, in the flickering firelight, she saw the demons dancing towards them, hundreds and hundreds of them waving knives and machetes and clubs.
'Quick, wake up,' she called, but no-one moved. In desperation she seized a burning log from the fire and dropped hot resin onto the men's feet—but still no-one stirred. Finally, just as the demons were nearly on top of them, she leaned across and bit her husband in the ear, hard! He woke with a yelp and, still half asleep, followed her to the tree the demon had pointed out.

Holding her baby in one arm, she managed to clamber up the trunk. Her husband came behind, tearing off the strips of bark as he went. Huddled together in the branches, they stayed safe and unmolested until morning.

When daylight came, they climbed cautiously down. The camp was deserted. Only the cold ashes showed that anyone had ever been there but a line of sinister tracks led from the fire to the cave entrance. The tribe had vanished completely. Though the woman and her husband called and searched all day, they found no sign of their people and no-one ever saw any of them again.

That is why, ever since that time, if you want to be safe from demons, you must wear a mask made from the bark of that special type of tree.

Tales of mischief and magic

The stories in this chapter come from the upper waters of the Paraguay river and from the great plains of central South America known as the Gran Chaco. The Gran Chaco stretches across Bolivia, southern Brazil, Paraguay and into northern Argentina. It is mainly dry scrub land and thorny, impenetrable jungle where trees rarely grow to more than ten metres high. Some parts have been cleared for agriculture but much of it is still very hostile country.

Several different groups of tribes live in the area and the stories here come from the Ayoreo, Tapui, Opayé, Bororo and Guarani tribes. The Ayoreo have only recently been discovered and live in the northern Chaco in east Bolivia and north-west Paraguay. The Tapui live on the Parapeti river south of the Rio Grande in east Bolivia. The Opayé come from the southern part of the Matto Grosso. The lands of the Bororo are around the upper waters of the Paraguay river. Living as hunters and working together to share the game they shoot and trap, the Bororo were until recently thought of as primitive savages. Their ceremonies and traditional ways of organizing their society were dismissed as nonsense by missionaries and traders and it is only in the last thirty or forty years that anthropologists are discovering the depth and complexity of their ideas.

The Guarani have survived much more successfully than most other South American Indians. In the seventeenth and eighteenth centuries Jesuit missionaries organized them into large, successful farming settlements in the fertile valleys between the Paraguay and Parana rivers. The settlements became very successful co-operative farms, growing oranges and the plant from which a drink called maté tea is made. Other settlers criticized the Jesuits for not preparing the Guarani for European civilization, resenting them because they prevented the Indians from being exploited as slave labourers. Eventually the missionaries were expelled and the farms fell into ruin—but the Indians survived. Although most of their culture and traditions have been forgotten, their language is now, with Spanish, an official language of Paraguay, spoken by 90 per cent of Paraguayans. Sadly, however, the Indians, who make up a large part of the population, are all too often simply workers on large estates and are no longer the legal owners of their traditional tribal lands.

How to use fire

The Opayé tell how the first owner and guardian of fire was the jaguar's mother. None of the other animals knew how to make fire and she kept it all to herself.

The armadillo was the first animal to try to steal fire from her. He went to the jaguar's mother's hut and politely asked her if he could warm himself for a while. She agreed and the armadillo sat down to wait for his chance. After a time she began to look drowsy and he began to tickle the soles of her feet with a feather. Soon she was snoring contentedly.

At once the armadillo snatched a burning twig from the flames and ran off as fast as he could. He did not get very far. As soon as he stopped tickling her feet, the jaguar's mother awoke and whistled a warning to her son the jaguar. He bounded off after the armadillo, snatched back the burning twig and ran home with it.

The next day a tapir decided to try his luck and trotted over to the jaguar's mother's hut. 'Good morning, grandmother,' he said. 'May I rest by your fire? I've been running from the hunters and I'm tired out.'

The jaguar's mother agreed and the tapir sat down very quietly. Soon the jaguar's mother fell fast asleep and at once the tapir snatched a burning twig and ran for the forest. Unfortunately as he ran out of the hut, he tripped on a tree root and crashed to the ground, waking the jaguar's mother. In no time at all she had whistled to her son and the tapir, like the armadillo, had lost his fire.

One after another all the animals tried to steal fire and one after another they failed. Each one managed to lull the jaguar's mother to sleep but she always woke up and called her son as soon as they left the hut. At last only one animal had not tried his luck, an animal rather like a large guinea pig, called a prea. The prea decided to try a different method of attack and instead of sending the jaguar's mother to sleep, he simply walked boldly into her hut and said, 'Good morning, grandmother. I've come for some fire.'

Before the jaguar's mother had time to realize what he had done, the prea had seized a burning log and trotted off quickly into the forest with it.

The jaguar's mother was so surprised that for some time she quite forgot to call her son and when she did, the prea was already some distance away. By twisting and doubling back on his tracks, he managed to keep just out of the jaguar's sight but at last, by the side of the Parana river, the jaguar caught up with him.

By now both animals were very tired and they sat down on the bank, panting hard. The prea recovered his breath first.
'Is fire really worth all this trouble?' he asked. 'Why don't you eat raw meat? It's much better for you than cooked food.'
'Is that so,' said the jaguar, looking hungrily at the prea. 'Then why do you want fire?'
'Well, I'd like to taste for myself what cooked meat is like,' said the prea innocently. 'Just once. How exactly do you prepare it?'
'If you are in a hurry,' said the jaguar, 'you just light a fire and put the meat on a stick and hold it in the flames until it turns brown. If you have more time you can dig a hollow in the ground and light a fire there. When it is really hot, you wrap the meat in leaves and put it in the hollow. Then you cover it all with hot ashes and earth and leave it to cook for several hours. That is really delicious.'

The jaguar loved explaining things and he talked for so long that by the time he had finished, the prea's burning log had grown quite cold. 'Don't worry,' said the jaguar kindly. 'It is easy to make fire.'

He showed the prea how to make a little heap of dry grasses and how to turn one stick against another until a spark flew and set the grass alight. 'Now you'd better go and find out what raw meat tastes like,' said the prea when he had learned all that he needed to know. 'I hope you like it.'

With that the two animals parted. The prea was so excited that he began to light new fires in every forest clearing. When he came to a village, he showed the people what to do to make fire and how to use it in the best way, and so he went from place to place, spreading the knowledge the jaguar had given him. Even today you can see black, charred circles in the forest which are the remains of some of his fires. As for the jaguar, he and his mother never ate cooked meat again.

The jaguar and the fox

A jaguar was hunting in the forest one day when he met a fox.

'I'm going to eat you,' said the jaguar.

'I don't taste very good,' said the fox. 'I think you'll be disappointed. Let me find you a nice fat ant-eater.'

The jaguar agreed and the fox led the jaguar to a part of the forest where the ant-eaters lived. The jaguar caught one easily and the fox watched hungrily as the jaguar ate the meat and gnawed the bones without even offering him a bone.

'Let me at least have the bladder,' said the fox at last and the jaguar grudgingly consented. The fox took the bladder and dried it out thoroughly in the sun. Then he blew it up like a balloon and caught some flies to put in it. He sealed the opening firmly and held it up to admire his work. The flies inside made a deep humming noise, like the sound of distant hunting dogs.

The fox crept silently up to the jaguar, who was sleeping heavily after his meal, and secretly tied the bladder to his tail. Then he poked the jaguar in the ribs and said, 'Listen, can you hear that noise? It sounds to me like a pack of dogs coming this way.'

The jaguar pricked up his ears and he, too, heard a humming noise which seemed to be coming from somewhere behind him. He stood up sleepily and began to lope off through the forest, leaving the fox grinning to himself. After a while the jaguar stopped to listen. The noise was still there; in fact it sounded to him as if it was even a little nearer. He ran on, faster now, deeper and deeper into the forest. Still the noise pursued him. At last he could run no more and he sat down to prepare himself for a fight. Only then did he turn to look at his tail and saw the fly-filled balloon buzzing away behind him.

'I'll get that fox,' he snarled furiously—but the fox was miles away in another part of the forest, gnawing the remains of the ant-eater bones.

The jaguar did not forget the trick that had been played on him and when he next met the fox he attacked him ferociously. 'This time I really am going to eat you,' he growled.

The fox, however, had a very persuasive manner. 'If you are as hungry as you look, you need more than a mere fox for dinner,' he said. 'Let me find you some nice fat human to eat. I'll show you where they walk and you can jump out on one.'

The fox led the jaguar to a clump of thick bushes by the side of a pathway that led to the river and the two animals lay down to wait, the jaguar poised to spring. They waited for a long time before the jaguar thought he heard someone coming.

'Let me have a look,' whispered the fox. 'You don't want to give away your position.'

The fox peered out from among the leaves and saw three young boys approaching.

'Can you see them?' asked the jaguar excitedly, sharpening his claws.

'Wait a minute,' said the fox. 'These are not yet men; they are not nearly fat enough for you.' And they settled down again to wait. After about an hour, the jaguar heard footsteps.

'Aha,' he said, 'here comes someone. His feet sound slower, he must be fatter.'

'Let me look,' said the fox. 'Oh, no, he won't do. This man has stopped being a man.'

An old, bent man came into view and the jaguar
sank back again, disappointed. An hour passed,
then another before the jaguar pricked up his ears.
'I hear someone.'
'Let me look,' said the fox. 'Oh yes, this one will
do nicely. Here is a fine juicy fat man for you. Get
ready now . . .'

If the jaguar had looked for himself he would
have seen that the man coming along the path was
indeed a fine, strong man; but he was also a fierce
hunter, carrying a well-used bow and arrows and
followed by three keen hunting dogs. However,
the jaguar was too busy arranging himself to
spring and was already licking his lips in
anticipation. As the hunter drew level with their
hiding place, the jaguar gave a loud roar and
launched himself into the air—only to find that
the hunter was too quick for him and had already
sent an arrow speeding towards him. Realizing at
last that he had been tricked again, the jaguar fled
howling into the forest with the three hunting
dogs panting behind him. As for the fox, he
grinned to himself and slunk away to find a new
victim.

The origin of honey

Wild honey is an important and delicious food to the forest Indians and they tell many stories about its origins. According to the myths, they believed at one time that it was not made by bees, but grew as the fruit of a special tree which could be cultivated like an ordinary food plant.

Once, the only animal who knew about honey was the wolf and he kept it all for himself and his children. They had more than enough to go round and you could see them smeared with it from early morning to late at night; yet he refused to give any to people outside his family. If they asked him outright for a taste, he simply gave them sweet fruits and pretended that these contained honey. As no-one knew for certain what honey was like, it was difficult to contradict him.

One day a small land tortoise decided it was time to discover the truth and, fitting his shell securely around him, he walked right into the wolf's den.
'I want some honey, please,' he said firmly.

At first the wolf denied he had any honey and made all kinds of excuses but the land tortoise simply repeated his request.
'All right,' said the wolf in the end. 'I have a large pot hanging up here. If you lie down on your back and open your mouth you can tip the pot with your toe and pour the honey into your mouth bit by bit.'

The land tortoise lay down and started to pour the honey into his mouth. He was soon totally absorbed in his delicious feasting. The wolf, however, did not intend to lose his secret food so easily. While the land tortoise lay helplessly on its back, he told his children to gather dry wood together and make a fire.
'Then we can have roast tortoise for dinner,' he told them gleefully.

The tortoise, drunk with sweetness, noticed nothing. He did not even notice when the flames started to lick around his shell, he just went on calmly eating, tipping the pot further and further over with his toe. Soon the heat was so great that even the wolf could not bear it and he had to go to stand outside. It was only when the land tortoise

had completely emptied the jar that he looked round, rolled himself over in the ashes and, scattering them on the floor, waddled out to find the wolf.

The wolf was astonished to see the land tortoise safe and well and when he heard him say calmly, 'You really must give some of that honey to the other animals,' the wolf fled away with his tail between his legs.

Now that the land tortoise knew the real taste of honey, he called all the other animals together and explained how wonderful it was. Determined to have their fair share, they set out to find the wolf and finally cornered him in a cave.
'Let's smoke him out,' they said. 'After all, he tried to do the same to you, tortoise.'

So they built a fire of brushwood which, aided by the wind, poured its smoke into the cave mouth. Just when the animals were wondering if they had killed the wolf by mistake, a partridge flew low through the smoke.
'That wolf is using powerful magic,' said the land tortoise. 'He has changed his shape to escape us—but he won't get far.'

Once again the animals set out. This time the chase lasted for days. Each time they thought they were within reach of the bird it flew off again, drawing them deeper into the forest. Then one day, as one of the animals stretched out its arm to catch the partridge, the bird changed its shape again and a little yellow and black bee zig-zagged up into the leaves.

By now the animals were becoming disheartened but the land tortoise persuaded them that the journey would soon be over and they continued to follow the bee. Before long they saw it disappear into a large hollow tree.
'Now we've got him. This is where the honey grows,' cried the land tortoise, and he started to poke his head into the tree. Suddenly he drew back with a shout. Buzzing angrily, an army of large, fierce wasps appeared in the entrance to the honey tree, threatening the animals with their stings. Some of the birds tried to rush the entrance but the wasps attacked, squirting them with a strange poison which made them fall back, stunned. Then the smallest bird of all, the hummingbird, dodged cunningly between the wasps, disappeared for an instant, and emerged

triumphantly, carrying honey in its beak. With its wings beating wildly, it hovered over the other animals, dripping the sweet liquid into their mouths.

Some of the animals were greedy and ate their share at once; but others took the honey carefully back to their homes and planted it like a seed in the ground. From each drop a new honey tree grew—and that is why today there is plenty of honey in the forest for everyone.

The origin of salt

The Ayoreo live today in the central part of the Chaco area, in Bolivia and Paraguay. For hundreds of years they remained isolated from outside influences, partly because of the difficult climate and country, partly because they were an extremely warlike and aggressive people. Today only some 2,500 of the Ayoreo survive. Many live in mission stations but some still follow their traditional hunting and gathering way of life in the jungle.

Salt deposits are common in the territory of the Ayoreo tribe, though for much of the year they lie hidden under pools of water. There was a time, however, when only one person, a woman named Sabaré, used any salt in her cooking. No-one else knew where it came from or how to use it, but everyone agreed that her food tasted better than anyone else's because it was salty.

Of course the other villagers tried very hard to find out her secret but she kept it well hidden and it seemed as if they would have to put up with their own tasteless food for ever. One day, however, a man called Cikenoi decided to spy on her as she cooked and, hiding himself in the corner of her hut, he watched as she prepared the vegetables and put them on the fire.
'Nothing unusual about that,' he thought, and indeed, everything seemed normal until right at the end when she took the pot off the fire; then she spat into it. 'Aha,' said the man to himself. 'So that's how she does it,' but though he told his wife what to do, their food still had the same bland taste as before.

After that, Cikenoi became quite obsessed with the woman's secret. He sat brooding about it for hour after hour until, in a jealous rage, he made up his mind to kill her. 'Why should she eat fine food when we have to put up with eating things that taste of nothing at all? She deserves to die,' he said. The next day he followed her when she went down to the river and killed her, leaving her body lying on the ground.

Cikenoi ran back to his home and at first told no-one what had happened. Soon, however, he began to feel guilty and he asked a friend to return with him to bury the body. As night fell, they crept up to the place where the woman had fallen. There, instead of her dead body, lay a heap of powdery crystals: her bones, her flesh, her whole body had turned to salt. Beside the heap of salt was a small pool of water which seemed to gleam in the moonlight and when Cikenoi and his friend tasted it, they recognized the flavour of the woman's food.

Ever since that day, the whole tribe has been able to find salt in the forests and have used it in their food whenever they cook.

The names of the stars

There was once an Indian of the Bororo tribe who took his little boy fishing and caught a large sting-ray. The little boy suddenly felt very hungry when he saw the fish so he asked his father to cook it for him. The man really wanted to continue fishing but he carefully built a fire and put the fish on to cook.
'You watch the fish and tell me when it's done,' he said. 'I'll come and take it off the fire for you.'

The father went on fishing while the little boy watched the fish cooking.
'It's ready,' he called, when the skin began to change colour in the flames, but his father waved back absent-mindedly, telling him to wait.
'Come on, come on,' called the boy. 'It's burning!' But still the father took no notice. He was on the track of another really large fish and there is nothing quite so absorbed as a fisherman in that situation.

The little boy decided to take the fish off the fire himself but its skin was so hot that it burned his

fingers and he tossed the fish into the air by mistake. Up flew the fish and landed right on the little boy's head. For a moment he was half blinded with the heat and the smoke.
'Aaah,' he cried, 'I'm burning.'

Then something strange happened. Perhaps it was a magic fish, perhaps the embers of the fire were enchanted, no-one will ever know, but mysterious sounds began to echo out of the forest. It was as if by throwing the fish in the air the boy had released some force which was now trying to communicate with him. He rushed to a nearby jatoba tree and jumped into its branches. 'Protect me, Grandfather tree,' he whispered, and the tree, which was also the home of spirits, heard him and answered in its own way. While the boy clung to its branches, it grew taller and taller until the ground was far, far away and even the tops of the other forest trees looked like a dark carpet of moss below him.

In the tree, the little boy lost all knowledge of time for he stayed there for months, perhaps even years, listening to the spirits of the tree. At night they talked to the stars in the dark sky. The tree spirits used a kind of whistle-language and the stars whistled back, telling the tree their names and their histories. Soon the boy learned to understand the sounds and he learned all their names and knew the stories of their lives.

One night, when the tree spirits were deep in conversation with the stars, the boy suddenly felt homesick for his father and mother and his ordinary village life. As the tree spirits were not taking any notice of him, he whispered softly to

the tree, asking it to grow small again so that he could jump down and run home.

Immediately, the ground was a few feet below him and the next minute he was scampering off to be welcomed as if from the dead by his parents.

The little boy never forgot his time in the trees and because he knew the names of the stars, he later became a very famous man. Sometimes, when the night sky was clear and the stars glowed in the blackness, he would stand by the jatoba tree and listen for the sounds of the spirits and the stars talking together. But he never heard them again.

Why you must not strike children

In the Chaco tribes it is very rare for a child to be hit by its parents—indeed, many families consider it criminal to do so. This story, told by the Tapui tribe, explains why.

One night there was a large party in the village and all the parents went to it. The children were safely locked in the huts while their parents enjoyed themselves but one little girl managed to climb out of the window and stole quietly along to the place where the party was being held. She stood peeping in at the window, watching the crowd of people drinking and dancing happily. Among them was her own mother, laughing wildly and swaying as she drank more and more of the strong maize beer.
'I never thought I would see my mother like that,' thought the little girl. 'Why is she staggering about?'

Just at that moment the mother raised her eyes and saw the little girl looking at her. 'I thought I told you to stay in the hut,' she shouted angrily, rushing out to see what was going on. Then, unable to bear the look in the little girl's eyes, she began to beat her, pushing her roughly back into the family hut with the other children. Satisfied that all was now secure, she staggered off back to the party, cursing and grumbling.

The little girl sat crying in the hut and, bit by bit, explained to the other children what had happened. She had never been beaten before and was angry and resentful. Suddenly, as if by magic, the locked door of the hut opened and all the

children in the house filed out into the moonlight. Holding each other by the waist, they formed a long line, softly chanting to themselves and stepping forward in short gentle steps to a rhythm which was quite unlike any that had ever been heard before. As they passed through the village, more and more children joined the line until every house was empty. Still singing their sad song the children danced out of the village, their eyes fixed on the sky, their steps becoming lighter and lighter until the leaders began to ascend slowly into the air. Up and up they rose, singing and dancing until they vanished into the darkness. In the places where they disappeared were bright new stars, some shining alone, some clustered together in little family groups, seeming to look down on the village below.

When the parents came home from the party, very late and very tired, the children were already far away in the night sky. Sadly the parents cried for the loss of their children, vowing never to ill-treat them again with either a harsh word or an angry gesture. To this day parents know that they must treat their children with great tolerance and understanding, remembering the village whose children became stars.

108

The jaguar's wife

Some women of the Opayé tribe were making a clearing in the jungle one day when one of them, a young girl, found the remains of an animal killed by a jaguar.

'I wish I were a jaguar's daughter,' she sighed. 'Then I'd have all the meat I ever wanted. Look, he has even left some here untouched.'

As she examined the carcass, she heard a low growl and there, in the grass, was the jaguar himself. 'Finding meat is easy,' he said. 'All you have to do is come with me. I promise I will never hurt you.'

The girl looked around to ask advice from the other women but they had all run away when the jaguar appeared, so she smiled at the jaguar and agreed to go with him. When the women returned they found no trace of her and assumed that she had been carried off and killed.

Then, one day, many months later, the girl returned to visit her family. She was looking well and happy and they crowded round to ask her what had happened.

'I married the jaguar,' she said, 'and now I have all the meat I want. In fact we have more than enough and he would be very happy to supply you with meat, too, like a good son-in-law. Now what kind of meat do you like?'

'Any meat will do for us,' they said.

'You must say what you prefer,' she insisted and they agreed to ask for tapir.

'Very well', said the girl. 'In the morning you will find all the tapir you need on the roof. You must make the roof posts strong enough to hold it all.'

Sure enough, the next morning the roof was covered with tapir meat, already cooked in the proper way. The family feasted on it until they could eat no more but two days later the same thing happened again. Soon the supply of meat became a regular occurrence.

After a time the jaguar began to grow tired of carrying meat from his lair to the village and he proposed, through his wife, that he should settle with her in the village. The family were still rather afraid of their son-in-law but they liked the meat so much that they agreed and the pair were given a hut at a safe distance from the family home. At first all went well. The jaguar's wife had become almost as skilled a hunter as her husband and there was more than enough food for all. Then one day the grandmother noticed that there was something strange about the girl. Black spots had started to appear on her body and when she held out her hands with the meat, her fingers looked remarkably like claws. Her feet, too, were changing and, although her face was as human as ever, her teeth seemed sharper and more fang-like than before. The grandmother said nothing but that night she prepared a powerful spell and the next morning the young wife was dead.

The family were secretly relieved at what had happened, but they were afraid of what the jaguar might do to them, and they offered him the girl's younger sister as a replacement wife.

'No, I want nothing from you,' said the jaguar calmly. 'I shall leave you and your village now, and no harm will come to you. Perhaps you will remember how I have behaved in the years to come.'

And the jaguar went off into the forest, roaring his disappointment and spreading fear throughout the forest; but the sound grew fainter and fainter as he went on his way.

Jokoramo the monkey

In the old days, the only living things on the earth were a monkey called Jokoramo, an oppossum, Kurugo, which he had reared from a cub and a parrot called Reko. They lived together in a small adobe hut, surrounded by a desolate wilderness.

Jokoramo's one treasured possession was a magic stick and one day when he felt particularly sad and alone in the world, he decided to use it to make some new companions. Striking it on the ground outside his hut, he said, 'Bring me some people.' Immediately a man of the white race appeared, a very tall and civilized person. 'Here I am,' he said.

Jokoramo struck the ground a second time and another civilized man appeared, this time with rather a red face. 'Here I am,' he said.

The third time Jokoramo used his wand an ugly, evil-looking man appeared, 'Here I am,' he grumbled. 'What do you want?'

The fourth time, a black man appeared, strong and handsome. 'Here I am,' he said.

Jokoromo made the Bororo tribe as his own special companions and continued naming and calling for race after race until the whole world was full of people. Soon, however, there were so many people of all shapes and sizes and colours that they started to jostle one another, complaining that they had not enough space to live comfortably, that there was nowhere to live and no shade from the heat of the sun.

Jokoramo, who was always a generous monkey, struck the ground again and suddenly there were trees of all kinds, and the earth became green. The white people immediately started to cut down the trees to make huts and soon they brought many houses together into towns and cities, dividing the land into states. When they began to complain that they had not enough to eat, Jokoramo gave them corn, sugar-cane, bananas and yams.

The white people prospered and Jokoramo saw that they were becoming more and more numerous every minute, spreading about all over the land. They built canoes and started to use the rivers; they even ventured out into the sea. At first they left Jokoramo and the land of the Bororo tribe alone but a time came when, forgetting what he had done for them, they raided his adobe hut and stole the magic stick for themselves.

When Jokoramo noticed that his magic stick was missing, he sent his parrot Reko to search for the white men along the banks of the river and set out himself with Kurugo his oppossum at his heels. It was not long before Reko found the men in a large canoe. Thinking that the parrot was bringing them more gifts from Jokoramo, the white men offered him a perch and crowded round him hopefully. While Reko distracted their attention with stories of Jokoramo's wonderful powers, Kurugo the oppossum slipped quietly onto the canoe and began sniffing his way around it, snuffling under the seats, peering into sacks and bundles, poking his nose into every hiding place. At last, among all the boxes of merchandise, he found the magic stick. With a satisfied grunt he took it in his mouth, slipped back overboard and made for the shore where Jokoramo was waiting. From his perch on the canoe, Reko saw what had happened and, breaking off in the middle of a most marvellous tale, flew away as fast as he could to join Jokoramo and Kurugo in the forest.

So the Bororo tribe took its magic back from the white man and has kept it safely ever since.

People of the great rivers

Between the Amazon and the Orinoco rivers and along the coast of Venezuela live tribes belonging to the Carib and Arawak races. These were the first American Indians that Europeans met, for they had colonized the islands in the Caribbean where Columbus landed in 1592. Today, the surviving groups of both races live on the mainland and very few remain on the West Indian islands.

According to history, the Caribs were a cruel and warlike race; our word 'cannibal' comes from a form of their tribal name. The Arawaks, who include tribes such as the Warao and Acawai, seem to have been gentler people.

Like the Amazon basin, the country around the Orinoco river is richly forested. According to W. H. Brett, who travelled in the Guyanas around the middle of the nineteenth century, 'the woods begin at the very edge of the sea and even in the sea, trees stand covered in leaves.' His description of the forest and its animals gives a vivid picture of the Indians' world:

'A dense forest spreads over many thousands of square miles, broken in places by swamps, in others by extensive savannahs, open tracks covered with grasses, with clumps of trees here and there. The sand-hills and ridges of moderate height near the Atlantic are covered by these immense forests; which extend to and climb the sides of the rocky mountains of the distant interior. Magnificent timber trees rear their heads above the smaller kinds, which fill the spaces between them, all struggling to find room for their foliage; while from a moist carpet of fallen leaves, moss, and fungi, springs humbler vegetation in rank luxuriance.

'Creepers and bush ropes as they are called, increase the difficulty of penetrating these dense forests. They ascend and descend, binding and interlacing trunks and branches in every direction. They sometimes destroy in their ever-tightening embraces the trees which support them; and large branches, even trunks, may be seen, half fallen with their descent arrested by them. The surface of the ground is strewed with dead leaves, fallen branches and trees in every stage of decay; some of which will crumble into dust beneath the feet.

'He who would see the beasts and birds of these forests should rise from his hammock and ramble with the Indian at early dawn, through the bush dripping with dew. The jaguar, having completed his nightly prowl, is retiring to his lair; the red howling monkey is uttering less terrible cries, beginning to tire of his own noise; the birds and smaller animals are coming out to feed and everything teems with life. High overhead green parrots, numerous as rooks or jackdaws, are flying to their feeding places. Macaws—blue and yellow, or blue and crimson—occasionally show themselves; The toucan or ''bill bird'' is displaying his gorgeous red and yellow breast, tossing his enormous beak with fantastic jerks on the top of the highest trees. Many others, beautiful in shape and colour, or good for food, may be heard if not seen. Least in size, but not in beauty, are the various species of humming-birds; flitting hither and thither like bees and flashing like jewels of many colours in the rays of the morning sun.

'Insects, creeping or flying, meet the eye in every direction. The huge black nests of the destructive wood ants are fixed on decaying trunks or branches. The coushi ants are stripping a tree, some nipping off the leaves above, while others below cut them into small pieces which thousands bear away to their nests deep in the earth. As you stand watching, the portions of green leaves seem to be moving along the tracks of their own accord. Other kinds of ants abound, as do butterflies and winged insects of innumerable species and large spiders which on every side are lurking to ensnare them.

'But the heat of the day increases and the birds seek shelter and repose. You may then hear in the distance the wood-pigeon's mournful call: and in certain districts the solemn toll of the snow-white campanero or bell bird resounds for miles over forest and river: but few birds disport themselves during the sultry noon, except the merry restless pai-pai-yo, which flits overhead from branch to branch and disturbs the general stillness by its strong clear note.

'When evening approaches, the busy scene of the morning is repeated. The mocking-birds, black and yellow or black and scarlet, become particularly noisy as they fly in and out of their hanging nests. The flocks of parrots noisily fly homeward and a large winged insect comes out as if to give notice of the close of day by a loud harsh noise. After this all gradually subsides into the stillness of night; broken by the croaking of frogs, the occasional cry of nocturnal birds, the chirping of insects and the slight sound of the vampire and other bats in their eccentric flight.'

The mythology of the Caribs and the Arawaks is very rich, full of forest stories and spirits. Perhaps the most popular figure is Makunaima, sometimes known as 'the great spirit' and Creator God, but at other times a mere trickster. He often appears as the younger of twins. Whereas his older twin is usually stupid, weak and lazy, Makunaima is lively and intelligent. In some stories the twins become personifications of the Sun and Moon, in others they are combined as one hero with two sides to his character. At one moment he can be dull and stupid, a dismal practical joker who has to be rescued from humiliation—at another a real friend to mankind.

To Europeans, one of the most famous legends of South America is the story of El Dorado, the Golden One. Deep in the interior, it was said, lay a fabulous city, so rich that the houses were plated with gold and the inhabitants sprinkled their bodies with gold dust as clothing. Some said that it had been founded by a member of the royal Inca race who had escaped from Spanish invaders. Expeditions from Spain, France and Portugal were all mounted to search for El Dorado and after exploring some of the Amazon country, the search moved to the land between the Amazon and Orinoco. Strong Indian tribes tried to destroy the invaders while weaker ones hurried them off their territory, raising false hopes by promising that the city was within easy reach. In 1595 Sir Walter Raleigh's English expedition found samples of gold-bearing quartz and one of his men described 'rocks shining with gold and a mountain containing diamonds and other valuable stones, the lustre of which is seen to blaze at a considerable distance.'

Some of the best clues about El Dorado come from Colombia but the city has never been found. The last major expedition took place in 1775–6 and ended, like those before it, in failure. Hundreds of hopeful travellers died either from disease or from hostile tribes and, it is said, only one man returned to tell the fate of his companions.

The tree of life

The Acawai tribe lived deep in the swampy region around the Orinoco River, remote from all contact with western civilization. In the middle of the nineteenth century this story of the creation of the world was still told by the old people as they lay in their hammocks around the glowing camp fires.

When the world began, the birds and animals were all created by Makunaima, the great spirit. In those days they could all speak like human beings and Makunaima put his son Sigu in charge so that they would live together in harmony. Every day the birds and animals went out to feed in the forests and each one brought Sigu the best food it could find, as a mark of respect and honour.

At first everyone depended on wild plants for their food for they knew nothing about digging and harvesting and the care of seeds and shoots. Then, one day, Makunaima ordered an enormous tree to spring out of the ground. Each of its branches produced a different kind of fruit while from around its trunk grew bananas, plantains and cassava, with maize and all kinds of corn. Yams and sweet potatoes also grew in clusters around its roots, for the great tree was the original stock from which all the cultivated plants of the world first came.

The agouti, trotting inquisitively about with his nimble, slender legs and bright black eyes, was the first to discover this great tree. He returned every day to feed there, selfishly eating all he could without telling the other animals anything about it. It was not long, though, before they noticed how sleek and fat he was growing and, seeing the remains of some strange fruit around his mouth, they determined to find out the truth.

Sigu commissioned the woodpecker to follow him. The woodpecker was a well-meaning and honest bird and it followed the agouti faithfully wherever it went. However, it was extremely fond of wood-ants and other insects which live under the bark of trees and it could not resist the temptation of examining every dry branch that lay in its path. The agouti soon noticed the continual tap-tapping sound which tracked him through the woods and he decided not to visit his secret tree that day.

The next day the rat was given the job and proved an excellent detective. He brought home samples of the best fruit and accused the agouti of greed in front of everyone. Ashamed, the agouti led the other animals to the tree so that they could all share in its riches. They rushed eagerly to it and began feeding at once, digging out the yams and potatoes, nibbling the maize and plucking the rich, ripe fruits. Quite soon it looked as if they would consume all the tree had to offer. Then Sigu decided it would be best to chop down the great tree and plant every seed and cutting they could take from it, so that the miraculous foods would be spread widely through the world.

Most of the animals helped willingly. Only Iwarrika, the monkey, was too lazy and tried to avoid his share of the work. Instead of helping, he continually interfered with the others and Sigu at last gave him a task which, he hoped, would keep him busy indefinitely: he sent him to fetch water from a stream, giving him only an open-work basket to carry it in.

When they had cut down the great tree, the animals discovered that its hollow stump was full of water. Swimming around in it were fresh-water fish of every possible kind. Up to that time, fish had only been found in the sea and Sigu decided to distribute these new fish to the streams, lakes and rivers of the land. This was not an easy undertaking. The water in the hollow tree was connected to an underground spring and now it began to bubble out, threatening to flood the land around. Quickly, Sigu made a magic basket of closely woven reeds and by placing this over the stump he managed to contain the water for a time.

It was Iwarrika, the monkey, who made trouble again. Tired of the thankless job he had been given, he crept back to the tree and saw the basket covering the stump.
'I suppose Sigu has hidden some of the best fruit there to eat when all the work is done,' thought Iwarrika. The temptation was irresistible and, making sure that no-one saw him, he pushed up the magic basket and peered inside. The next instant he was gasping and struggling in terror as a great torrent of water burst out and rushed out

over the countryside in a roaring tidal wave.

Led by Sigu, the birds and animals made for the highest hill they could find. A group of tall cocorite trees grew there and Sigu urged the birds and climbing animals to perch as high as they could in the branches. The amphibious animals were safe enough and Sigu placed the rest in a cave with a very narrow entrance, which he sealed with wax so that the water could not enter. First, however, he gave the animals inside a long thorn which they could use to pierce the wax and discover when the water level had gone down. Then he joined the other birds and animals at the very top of one of the cocorite palms.

Many terrible days and nights of darkness and storm followed. The animals clung to their perches, cold, wet and hungry. All this time Sigu waited with them, from time to time dropping seeds from the cocorite tree down into the water below. At first he heard them splash into the water almost immediately but as time passed, they took longer and longer to reach the surface. Then at last they all heard not a splash but the dull sound of seeds striking soft earth. At the same moment the sky grew lighter and the birds began to sing to welcome the dawn once more.

As the flood subsided, the seedlings and cuttings that the animals had planted sprang to life just as Sigu had planned. His distribution of the fresh-water fishes, however, was not quite so successful. As the water flooded out of the tree stump they were carried out with it and, left to themselves, they settled into the new rivers and streams very unevenly so that some rivers still contain a great variety of fish while others have few if any of the best kinds.

And what happened to the monkey who had caused all this havoc? He was certainly not cured of his idle ways, or of his love of mischief and thieving, for he handed those qualities down quite unimpaired to his children. He seems, however, to have acquired a great horror of water, a horror which his descendants, after all these years, still share.

The sky people

The Warao tribe now live as hunters and gatherers in the swampy Orinoco delta. Some anthropologists believe, however, that they migrated there from territory to the west of their present lands, perhaps driven out by a stronger tribe.

According to their own ancient beliefs, the original home of the Warao was not on this earth at all, but in a place above the sky. In that world they were always happy for there were no dangerous animals and no wicked people to trouble them. The young hunters spent their time pursuing beautiful, brightly coloured birds, whose feathers they used as clothes and ornaments.

One day a hunter named Okonorote had wandered a long way from his village, following a particularly fine bird. He was searching for an arrow which had missed its mark when he found a hole in the ground through which the arrow had apparently fallen. Peering down, he saw the lower world stretched out beneath him, with herds of bush-hogs, deer and other animals feeding and roaming undisturbed through green forests and plains. Judging that the hole was large enough for him to pass through, he twisted a long rope from cotton and, with the help of friends, lowered himself carefully down.

The friends waited around the hole for several days and at last Okonorote came struggling back up the rope, full of stories about the unlimited food and an easy life below. The people were easily persuaded and soon they were climbing one by one through the hole, first the young men, then the elders of the villages, the children and the wives. All, that is, except the very last wife who was too fat to squeeze through the hole and remained stuck fast in the narrow opening, filling it completely. It was impossible to help her from below and, since there was no-one left above to pull her out, there she was forced to stay, cutting off all hope of return for the rest of the tribe.

The Warao found that the new lower world was as full of game as Okonorote had promised, but that water was very scarce. Accordingly, the Great Spirit created the Essequibo river for general use and a small lake of fresh, sweet water which, he commanded, was to be used only for drinking, never for bathing or washing.

For many years the orders of the Great Spirit were carefully obeyed and all went well for the Warao tribe. Then one day a family of four brothers and two sisters came to live by the lake. The sisters, Korobona and Korobonako, were beautiful but headstrong girls who had little respect for the traditions of their elders. As soon as they knew they were forbidden to bathe in the lake, they longed to do so more than anything else and early one morning, they waded out into its clear water. In the very centre of the lake was a pole which, they knew, was sacred. The boldest of the two reached out to give it a shake, sending wide ripples racing to the shore. As she touched it, the charm which had held the spirit of the water was released and he seized her firmly by the hand and dragged her down to his watery home. The other girl fled home and, though she was dripping wet, would say nothing of what had happened.

Three days and three nights passed before Korobona returned home. She, too, said nothing about her experiences. The result, however, was impossible to hide, for after a few months it was obvious that she was going to have a baby. Angrily the brothers demanded to know who the father was and at last she confessed that it was the water spirit himself.
'What kind of a monster will come from such a father?' they shouted but when the baby was born and appeared in every way like a human child, they relented. The baby was allowed to live and grow up with them and Korobona's crime was forgiven.

Korobona could not forget the clear, clean water of the pool, and she longed to see the mysterious water spirit again. After a while she secretly visited him once more—and again she bore him a child. This time, however, only its head and body were those of a boy; from its waist down it was a python, covered in variegated scales. Korobona had given birth to her child in the deep forest and there she hid him, cherishing him secretly, carrying him food when her brothers were not looking.

Eventually, however, they discovered her terrible secret and, creeping up on the serpent child while it was asleep, they shot it with their arrows and left it for dead. When Korobona went to her child that night, she found it barely alive but with her love and care she revived it and before long it had grown to a frighteningly large size.

Again the brothers decided to destroy it but this time, knowing that it had increased in strength and would regard them as enemies, they assembled all the weapons at their command. Bristling with knives and arrows they attacked and, though Korobona tried to shelter the monstrous child with her own body, they succeeded in hacking it to pieces.

Sadly, Korobona collected the remains of the serpent child together and covered them with a heap of fresh leaves. Every day she sat beside them and after many days and nights, her patience was rewarded. The heap of leaves began to rustle and move and from it an Indian warrior slowly arose. He was a majestic and terrible figure. His forehead was painted red and he was armed with bow and arrows, fully equipped for battle.

This mighty warrior was the first Carib, the father of a powerful race. His first task was to avenge the serpent-child from whose dead body he had sprung and, striding through the forest, he drove the brothers and their fellow Warao tribesmen before him, deeper and deeper into the swamps. His descendants, a race of sons as grave and terrible as their father, continued to harass the Warao until at last they were driven to the shores of the ocean itself, never to return to the pleasant hunting grounds they had visited from the sky.

Why honey is scarce now

Like other forest tribes, the Arawak Indians valued honey and those who collected it highly. In the old days there were many bees' nests in the bush and it was easy to find plenty of honey. One man in particular always seemed to know where the best honey trees were. Every day he strode off into the forest, his axe over his shoulder. Treading softly on the thick carpet of leaves, he glanced around him, watching the insects in the brilliantly coloured flowers, noting the

holes and crevices in the bark of the trees. He was chopping into a hollow tree one day when he heard a shriek of pain.

The man was very surprised and he enlarged the hole in the tree very gently until he could see right inside. There stood a beautiful woman. 'My name is Maba,' she told him. 'I am the spirit of honey, the honey mother. I was just inspecting these bees' store when you nearly cut me in two.'

As Maba had no clothes, the man ran off to fetch some cotton from a silk-cotton tree and she deftly twisted it into a suitable cloth. Only then did he feel he could talk to her properly. The first thing he did was to ask her to marry him and she agreed.

'You must remember one thing, though,' she added. 'You must never, never mention my name out loud. If you do, I shall have to leave you, whether I want to or not.'

The man promised to be most careful and tried never to think of her name so that he could not even mention it in a moment of distraction or absent mindedness. He decided to call her simply 'Wife'.

The pair lived happily together for many years. The wife was a good cook and made excellent cassiri and paiwarri, beers made with manioc and sweet red potatoes. No matter how many visitors came to the house, one jugful of her beer would make them all gloriously drunk and their parties were famous far and wide. The man became even better at finding honey and he, too, became well known and respected for his skill.

One day, however, he was drinking with a group of friends. Everyone was flushed and merry and they had drained the last drop from the jug of cassiri.

'Never mind,' said the man, 'Maba will make some more.'

No sooner had he said her name than, tipsy as he was, he realized his mistake. As he rose to his feet in alarm, a tiny bee flew out of the hut, straight past his head. It circled once, and though he reached out imploring hands to stop it, disappeared into the jungle. Maba had left him forever.

With Maba all the man's luck and happiness flew away—and somehow there was never much honey to be found from that time onwards.

The story of Adaba

There were once three Arawak brothers who set out on an expedition with their sister to look for game. They had been without meat for several days in the village and hoped to find suitable animals more easily in a new area. They built a hunting camp in the jungle and left the sister to look after the fire while they wandered off to look for food.

It happened that a tree-frog named Adaba lived near the place where they had built their camp. His home was in a hollow tree where a pool of rainwater had collected and he was splashing happily there, singing to himself when the girl called out to him: 'Oh do stop making that noise. You may feel pleased with life but I shan't be happy until I've had a good meal—and that's not likely to happen to me tonight.'

Adaba stopped singing and looked at the girl, who was trying to make soup out of some bitter vegetables. He decided to help her and, as he was a magic tree-frog, turned himself quickly into a man and went off into the bush to hunt. Two hours later he returned loaded with meat which he told the girl to cook; the brothers, he suspected, would not bring back much.

He was right. All the brothers had managed to catch was an old, scraggy wild turkey so they were pleasantly surprised to see the fire glowing under chunks of tender meat. They also saw a strange man lying in one of their hammocks, looking very much at home. And he *was* strange: he had stripes all the way down his thin legs and his eyes bulged almost out of his forehead. However, they greeted him politely and exchanged the usual courteous enquiries. 'Have you had good hunting?' asked Adaba.

The brothers held up their feeble catch, ashamed to be seen as such poor providers. 'Let me see your arrows,' went on Adaba. He inspected them carefully, then burst into laughter. 'I'm surprised you can hit even a tree trunk with these. Look, they have fungus growing on them. They will never shoot straight.' He handed them a bunch of soft leaves and showed them how to clean the arrows correctly. 'Now,' he said. 'Tie a fishing line between the branches of these two trees. Good. Now stand back and fire your arrows at the line.'

To their amazement, the brothers succeeded in shooting their arrows straight through the taut line. Regarding him with new respect, they invited Adaba to stay. The next day he taught them a new way to shoot by aiming the arrow into the air so that it fell vertically down into an animal's neck. Then he taught them how to stalk silently through the undergrowth, how to track their prey by a thousand secret signs and how to lie motionless for hours, waiting to attack.

Under his guidance, the brothers became excellent hunters and they decided to take him back to their village as their brother-in-law. Their sister was pleased to marry and Adaba was accepted into the group. For many months hunting went well and the village people grew sleek and healthy.

Then one day Adaba's wife said, 'Come and bathe with me in the river, Adaba.'
'No, I can't,' he replied. 'You know I don't like the river. The only place I can bathe is in the water hole in the hollow tree.'
'Well, then, come and watch me instead,' she said.

Reluctantly, Adaba followed her to the river and stood rather timidly on the bank. His wife laughed at him. 'What a coward you are,' she cried. 'It's lovely in the water.' Then she splashed him three times, laughing and teasing him.

As soon as the water splashed onto his body, Adaba began to shiver and shake.
'Whatever's the matter?' asked his wife, alarmed, and she began to clamber out of the muddy river. Before she could reach him, however, his body had dwindled and shrunk until he had changed back into a small, long-legged tree-frog and was hopping as fast as he could for the hollow tree. 'Adaba,' she wailed. But he was gone.

When the three brothers returned at the end of the day and asked for Adaba, the wife said sadly that he had gone away and although they questioned her all night, she would say no more.

Adaba never came out of his hollow tree again and hunting was never as good in the village as it had been in his day. Only his wife knew that he was still living nearby and in the evenings she would often sit sadly by the hollow tree, listening to the tree-frog's song.

The far south

The extreme tip of South America lies less than 800 miles from the continent of Antarctica. The cold, stormy climate brings snow and ice to the mainland for much of the year and glaciers are a common sight in the channels among the offshore islands. The Yamana or Yaghan Indians, whose stories are in this chapter, used to live on the islands off the south coast of Tierra del Fuego but have now become so scattered that it is no longer possible to identify them as a tribe. Like the other peoples of the region, they lived traditionally by fishing and travelled mainly by canoe. Mussels, seals and porpoises made up their diet while an occasional whale, thrown up on the shore by the storms, provided them with a feast of meat. Their stories, full of the birds and animals of the cold south, reflect their close relationship with a bleak and hostile environment.

According to Yamana tradition, their ancestors were two Suns, an older and a younger, the Moon and her husband the Rainbow. They all came to live in the Yamana country and there created the first Yamana people. In the old days, the women ruled over the men, keeping them in subjection by pretending to be spirits. Hanuxa, the Moon, was the leader of the women. Rainbow's brother, Younger Sun, was a great hunter and one day he led the men in a revolt against the women. In the battle all the women were killed except Hanuxa; she fled up to the sky and took her place as the Moon. You can still see the scars she received in the fight on her face today. Younger Sun pursued her but, unable to capture her, took his place as the Sun. Older Sun turned into a star, the planet Venus. Rainbow, unwilling to forsake the earth completely, came and went between the land and the sky. Hanuxa had escaped but she was still angry with the people on earth and in revenge for the death of the women, she jumped with all her force into the sea, causing a terrible flood which swept over the whole land.

Many Yamana stories are about the hero twins, the Yoalux brothers, who were among the first men to return to the land after the flood. Their adventures were often told to explain the origins and importance of social customs and the need to learn and use hunting skills. Like the tales of animals and spirits given in this chapter, they were recorded before the tribe was scattered; through them the outline of Yamana tradition has been preserved.

The cormorants

The Wollaston Islands are among the most southerly islands off the coast of South America and lie next to Cape Horn itself. One hard winter, a woman found herself alone on one of the tiny patches of land. Her hut was cold and damp because she had no firewood left to burn and she had very little to eat. She was lying one night in the corner of her hut, unable to sleep for cold and hunger, when she saw a large black bird fly in and settle down in the middle of the floor. Soon another bird joined it and, to the woman's surprise, they began to talk to each other in the language of the Yamanas.

'How strange,' thought the woman and, raising her head she saw that there were now several more birds in the room and that they were sitting around a fire which they had lit, shivering with cold. The woman moved closer so that she could hear what they said more clearly, crouching unseen in the shadows.

The birds were discussing the long journeys they had taken, how they had flown out over the open sea, of the harbours they had visited, the fish they had captured and the dangers they had escaped. As they grew warmer, the birds talked and laughed more freely and the woman understood everything they said.

'How nice to have someone to talk to at last,' she said. 'Perhaps they are not really birds at all,' and she moved even closer, longing to join in the conversation, to warm herself at the flames and to tell them of the long, lonely winter she had spent. As she came out of the shadows she saw that the birds were all busy scraping and cleaning skins and, in her eagerness to push into their circle, she bumped one of them with her arm. Then the birds saw her clearly in the light of the fire and, taking fright, immediately snatched up their skins, beat out the fire with their wings and flew out into the night. 'But I only wanted to talk,' she wailed after them. 'Come back, birds.' It was too late, they were gone.

The birds had scattered the ashes of their fire but they had left behind a large part of a whale's carcass which was too heavy for them to carry. The woman now had plenty of food but she was still lonely and cold and she longed for the sound of her language and for the company of friends around the fire. She sat crying in the darkness for days, and as the hours passed her voice seemed to grow shriller and her small, hungry body to shrink away. At last she could cry no more and, staggering to her feet, she walked awkwardly to the door of the hut. Suddenly she no longer felt cold and sad and, looking down she saw that her body was covered with soft, sleek feathers and that her arms had changed to powerful wings. Far out over the sea she could hear the birds calling to one another and, with a cry of recognition, she let the wind lift her into the air and flew off over the waves to join her new companions.

The sparrow shaman

Once, long ago, a whale was stranded and died on the southern coast. The nearest villagers lit four great fires to call people from all around to share in the feast and very soon a large crowd had gathered. Among them was a powerful shaman named Hespul the Sparrow who arrived with his own group of followers. Everyone was preoccupied with cutting and distributing the whale meat and blubber and, although they welcomed the newcomers in a friendly way, they gave Hespul no special attention.

Hespul was deeply offended by the people's behaviour but he said nothing at the time. Instead he began to brood about the insult and to plan his revenge. A few days later, when the sun was at its highest point in the sky, he worked his powerful magic and brought a great darkness over the whole land.

The terrified people were asking each other where the darkness had come from when suddenly a voice said, 'It is I, Hespul, the great shaman, who sent the darkness. Now, perhaps you will recognize me and treat me with the respect I deserve.'
'How long will it last?' asked the people.
'It will last forever,' replied Hespul.

The people begged and pleaded with Hespul, explaining how they would die of hunger if they could not find food, offering to give him the choicest pieces of meat and blubber and to give him all the honour a shaman could demand. 'We did not know you,' they said, 'but now there is no doubt that you are the greatest shaman in the world. Take away your darkness and we will always honour you.'

For a time Hespul remained stern and angry but at last he relented and agreed to reverse his magic. With great ceremony, he rubbed white paint on his body and painted a red line across his face. Then, putting on his sparrow feather head-dress, he turned slowly round and began to sing his song of the east. As he chanted it began to grow lighter and, very slowly, the day returned.

Only when it was bright day once more did the people sigh with relief and prepare a feast in his honour.

Hespul, the sparrow, still chants his song of the east and his 'pit, pit, pit' notes can be heard every morning welcoming the sun. Since the days when Hespul was insulted, however, the dawn comes very slowly, to remind people of his power over light and darkness, night and day.

The magic ibis

It had been a long, hard winter in the cold southern lands at the tip of the continent and it seemed to the people that this year spring would never arrive. Then, one morning, an old man looked out of his hut and saw a large, rusty brown bird flying high overhead, heading southwards towards the sea.
'The ibises are here,' he called. 'Look, spring is coming.'

Everyone ran out of their huts, pointing to the sky, shouting and laughing like madmen.

Now the ibis was a very sensitive bird and liked to be treated with gentle respect, not with loud, sudden noises, however welcoming they were intended to be. When she heard the screams of the villagers and saw them dancing and running around, she was deeply offended. To show her feelings, she decided to delay the spring they were already celebrating and plunge the country once more into winter.

The cold she sent was worse than anything they had experienced before. First there was a sudden snowstorm, followed by a frost which seemed to penetrate into their very bones. For months on end, snow fell every day and the land was soon completely covered with hard-packed snow, frozen at night under a glittering sheet of solid ice. The water froze in the streams and many people died because they could not dig their canoes out to go in search of fish. The people huddled together in their huts, short of firewood and food, barely surviving.

At last the ibis relented. The snow stopped and the sun shone once more, melting the ice and snow so that the rivers and streams were swollen with rushing water. The sun burned so fiercely down on the mountain tops that it scorched their thin soil and nothing new could grow there; to this day the mountains have bare, rocky summits. Soon the people were able to dig out their canoes and gradually life began to return to normal.

Only on the mountain slopes and in the deep valleys the ice remained, too thick to melt in the short summer, a heavy permanent covering that remains in places to this day. And in the channels between the islands, towering icebergs still float, the broken remains of the ice sheet that the ibis brought.

Since that time, the Yamana Indians have always treated the brown ibis with respect, although they still regard her arrival as a sign that spring is on the way. Now they are quiet when they see her fly round their huts, the children are kept indoors and no-one really believes that winter is over until she has passed safely by.

The cannibals

There was once a family of Yamana Indians who lived on the shore near what is now Usuaia. One day a rumour started to spread through the village that, far to the west, a whale had swum ashore and was stranded. 'They say there is good meat and blubber for everyone,' said their neighbour. 'Don't be left behind.'

The next day the family set out in their canoe, taking with them the village shaman. They paddled day and night in their anxiety to reach the whale as quickly as possible but, unfortunately, the night was so dark that they paddled right past the place where the whale lay. In the morning they found themselves in an unfamiliar country, right outside the territory of the Yamana. Seeing a large settlement, they decided to land and find out where they were and what had happened to the whale.

What the family did not know, however, was that the people in this country were cannibals. It was their custom to welcome strangers from the east and offer them lodging for the night, one person to each hut. Having separated them, it was easy for the cannibals to overpower the strangers one by one at their convenience.

The family was, accordingly, made welcome and when evening came they were each shown to their separate lodgings. The shaman, too, was given a place to stay. When he arrived there, he found an old woman sitting by the fire making a basket. Her husband was cooking something over the flames and the shaman saw to his horror that it was a human leg.
'Like some supper?' said the man.
'Certainly not,' said the shaman. 'I will never eat human flesh, however hungry I may be.'

The shaman ran out of the hut and went down to the shore to look for a fish to eat and, still not realizing what the cannibals planned, he returned to the hut to sleep. He was quietly eating his fish when he noticed a group of children in the corner of the hut. They were jumping up and down excitedly, pointing to him and chattering in a language the shaman could not understand. In fact they were saying: 'Let's eat the stranger today, we're hungry.' And the parents were replying calmly, 'No, we'll save him until tomorrow. Be patient, we have enough for tonight.' However, the children continued to clamour and point, licking their lips in a menacing way until at last the shaman realized that he was destined to be their next meal.
'We are all in danger,' he thought, 'and I alone can save the family.'

Stealthily taking a special piece of fat from his bag, he threw it onto the fire. Immediately a dense smoke filled the hut and the cannibals fell deeply asleep under its magic influence. The smoke spread from hut to hut until all the people of the settlement were unconscious. Only the Yamana were left awake. Then the shaman ran from hut to hut, calling his people to leave at once and, taking as many of their evil hosts' belongings as they could carry, they jumped into their canoe and paddled away as fast as they could.

They had already paddled some distance when a dog began to bark in the village and the cannibals awoke. Angry that both their next meal and their belongings had vanished, they set off in pursuit. The Yamana family had only a small canoe, now heavily loaded with stolen goods, and the cannibals soon began to draw nearer and nearer. 'We shall have to hide,' advised the shaman, and with an enormous effort, they managed to paddle round a rocky headland out of sight of the pursuers. Scrambling hastily ashore, they hid themselves among the rocks on the shore. They were not safe there for long. The cannibals climbed the hills behind to get a view over the ocean and began to throw rocks down on the cowering Yamana. The rocks exploded with great violence as they hit the shore, making the same thundering noise that you can still hear in those regions today; only now, they say, it is caused by icebergs colliding in the channels.

Taking to their canoe again, the Yamana sped away, throwing their stolen goods overboard to lighten the load, paddling like men possessed. At last they reached the borders of their own country again and the cannibals gave up the chase.

The Yamana were careful not to stray so far to the east again and they know, now, when they are nearing the dangerous area; in those parts you can still see the rocks littering the shore where the cannibals threw them down.

Tales of the southern plains

South of the Gran Chaco, the land changes gradually to become the flat, grassy pampas of Argentina, Patagonia and Chile. East of the Andes lived tribes such as the Puelche of Argentina and the Tehuelche of Patagonia. The Tehuelche are tall people, the men averaging over 1·8 metres in height, and they were frequently described by early travellers as a race of giants. Once hunters of plains animals such as rheas and guanacos, their descendants are now often gauchos on the great Argentinian cattle ranches.

The stories in this section come from the Mapuche tribe, a branch of the Araucanian Indians who once inhabited much of the southern Andes region, from the Pacific to the Patagonian plains. They were divided into four groups: the Pichunche (north people); the Huilliche (south people); the Pehuenche (people of the pines); and the Mapuche (people of the land). Unconquered by the Incas, they also fought fiercely against the Spanish and the farming branch of the tribe, the Mapuche, were never really defeated. It was not until the last century that they were subdued and, although there are now under half a million pure Mapuche, their heroic resistance to foreign invasion has made them justly famous.

One reason why the Spanish could not enslave the Mapuche was that many Spanish people chose to live among the Indians and to adopt their ways. We often forget that the civilizations of many Indian races were equal to if not superior to European ones and it is not surprising that Spaniards who were taken captive in wars or guerrilla raids should choose to stay with their captors.

Some Mapuche stories are obviously influenced by foreign traditions but their creation stories seem firmly linked to a more ancient culture. They believe that every seventy thousand years, the earth collides with another world and everything is destroyed. Then the gods start creation anew. Like other Indian peoples, they have a flood story, this time involving a fight between two serpents. The present tribe, they say, came from the Sun and Moon, who once sent their rays to earth in the shape of a strange stone figure. At the same time another ray struck a cleft in the volcano called Pillan and from this walked the man and woman who were to become worshippers of the man of stone and parents of the Mapuche tribe.

The three pledges

There was once a young man called Namuncura
who fell in love with a beautiful Indian girl, the
daughter of a Mapuche chief. He possessed
nothing in the world except three gold chains, of
which he was very proud. He was much too poor
to approach the girl's family as an official suitor
but one day, desperate with love, he went to her
and showed her one of his chains.

'I love you very much,' he said, 'and I know I am
too poor to marry you. But look: if you will let
me sleep at your feet for just one night, I will give
you this golden chain.'

The chief's daughter always had plenty of girl
attendants sleeping in her room so she knew she
would come to no harm and, since she liked the
golden chain, she agreed. That night Namuncura
slept at her feet, contented simply to be near her.

The next day he offered her the second chain on
the same condition and again the girl agreed. On
the third day he offered her the third chain and
that night he slept a third time at her feet.

The girl was impressed by the poor man's love
and respect and when he at last dared to propose
marriage to her, she accepted. 'But keep it secret
for the time,' she begged. 'I must explain it to my
father.'

'Very well,' said Namuncura. 'We will not marry
yet and I will tell no-one of our plan. But in
exchange I want you to wait for me for three years
while I go to make my fortune. If you are to be my
wife I must be rich and powerful, a fitting
husband for a chief's daughter.'

'How do I know that you will come back?' asked
the chief's daughter.

'I shall take from you three pledges,' said
Namuncura. 'These will bind us together forever.'

The girl gave him three of her best clothes, a
skirt, a blouse and a shawl and, packing them
carefully, he set off to make his fortune.

Three years later, Namuncura did indeed
return as a rich young man, full of stories of his
adventures. Elegantly dressed, he had the look of
a man who has travelled far and learned many
things. He rode immediately to the village where
the chief's daughter lived, eager to share his good
fortune with her. When he arrived he found a

crowd of gaily dressed people, obviously ready for a celebration and when he inquired what was happening he was told that on that very day the chief's daughter was to be married. Concealing his distress, Namuncura mingled with the guests. 'You're a stranger here aren't you?' asked the chief, admiring Namuncura's fine horse. 'From the look of your clothes and the fine harness on your horse, you must have come far. Won't you dismount and tell us about yourself? My daughter is getting married today to a fine rich landowner I have selected for her and it would be most entertaining if you would tell us your adventures while we are waiting for the ceremony to begin.'

'Certainly, if you are interested,' said Namuncura politely, and he sat down in front of the chief's house, surrounded by an eager circle of listeners. As they gathered round, the chief's daughter herself appeared in the doorway of the house and Namuncura's heart leaped: she was as beautiful as ever, though her eyes, he saw, were sad. She looked at him without recognizing him. In his fine clothes, with the beard he had grown while he was away, and his hat pulled down over his face, he looked like any other stranger to her.

'The first and best thing that happened to me was that I earned enough to buy three fast hunting dogs,' he began. 'They brought me all the luck in the world. I was riding on the pampa one day when I saw a fine rhea running in front of me. It had such fine plumage that I longed to catch it, so I sent one of the dogs after it at once. The dog was fast, but how that rhea ran! I've never seen anything to match it and the dog had no chance at all of overtaking it. At last, however, the dog managed to snap at its tail feathers—and look what fell off.'

Namuncura held up the skirt that the chief's daughter had given him as a pledge. The crowd roared with laughter at the idea of a rhea with a skirt and the girl looked at the man with new interest.

'Well then,' continued Namuncura, 'I could see that the first dog was finished, so I sent the second one after the bird. I was really determined to get its feathers. This dog was even faster than the first and it soon drew level with the rhea. With a great bound it just managed to nip one of the bird's wings. The rhea shook the dog off, though, and

ran on. But it dropped something else this time.'

Namuncura held up the blouse, the second pledge, to show the crowd. Again they laughed and again the girl stared at the young stranger with wide eyes.

'I wasn't going to give up that bird for anyone,' continued Namuncura, 'and I could see it still in the distance, peacefully feeding. I crept nearly up to it before it noticed me, then I sent the third dog off. Away they went, streaming like water over the sands and this time I knew the bird was mine. In no time the dog had brought the great bird to the ground and as it fell, it dropped this.' Namuncura held up the shawl, the third pledge. 'So then . . .'

'Stop,' cried the girl, 'You don't need to say another word. You are my real love and my real husband and those are the pledges I gave you three years ago, to make sure you would return. I claim them and you for my own.'

The chief, impressed as he already was by Namuncura's prosperous appearance, gave his consent to the marriage and even the disappointed landowner could not oppose the girl's wishes. So the young man who had started with nothing but three gold chains won his heart's desire.

The lost lovers

There are many stories in Mapuche mythology about lost towns and villages, their houses buried beneath earth or sand, or drowned under the sea. One of the most famous tells of a city hidden in the mountains by the side of a mysterious lake. On one side is a hill of diamonds, on the other a hill of gold. There is a temple in the city whose bell, when it is rung, can be heard all over the world. The inhabitants of the city are tall and fair and none of them ever dies. The city is surrounded by a dense mist which means that no stranger can find it, but if anyone does stray inside its walls, they forget the world outside and never return to it again.

Not all the lost places were as rich and powerful as the mysterious mountain city. Some, like the village in this story, were humble fishing villages, perhaps overwhelmed long ago by the Pacific storms, buried under the drifting sand.

There was once a poor fisherman called Curi-Caven, or Black Thorn, who lived in the village of Pelluhue in southern Chile. He married a beautiful Indian girl and they had a little daughter, Rayen-Caven, or Thorn Flower. When Thorn Flower was still a baby, her mother died leaving the husband to bring up the child as best he could. Thorn Flower grew up almost an orphan. Her father had to fish all day long—and often in the night as well—to keep them both alive and she was left very much alone. Black Thorn could never forget his beautiful young wife and even when he was at home he was silent and depressed, taking no notice of the growing child.

One day, when Black Thorn was sitting in deep despair, wondering what to do, a Sea Spirit appeared at the door of his hut.
'Your daughter is growing up wild and quite untrained,' said the Sea Spirit, 'and I can see that you do not know what to do. Listen. I will look after her for you and see that she is well educated in all the skills a girl should know. Then, when she is twenty years old, I shall claim her as my bride. Do you accept?'

The poor fisherman had little choice. He knew he could not teach the girl himself and there was no-one else to help them. Reluctantly, he agreed to the Sea Spirit's terms.

From that day on, little Thorn Flower began to change. She learned how to spin and weave and sew, how to cook and clean, to do all the things that a young girl learns from her mother—and all apparently without anyone to guide her. When her father asked who taught her, she replied, 'Oh, I just know that is how to do it,' and went on with her work. Black Thorn grew more cheerful and even his fishing seemed to prosper. He said nothing to Thorn Flower about his pact with the Sea Spirit and, indeed, almost forgot about it himself.

Then, one day, Thorn Flower brought a young Indian to visit and explained that they had fallen in love and wished to marry. The boy, called Necul-Narqui, or Quick Cat, seemed suitable in every way: he was young and handsome and had enough money to support Thorn Flower in her own home. But Black Thorn was doubtful.
'Perhaps the Sea Spirit has forgotten,' he said to himself. 'It is all so long ago. But if he comes, I cannot break my side of the bargain. Well, I'll say nothing to Thorn Flower yet. Let's wait and see.'

The couple were to be married on Thorn Flower's twentieth birthday and just a week before the day, the Sea Spirit appeared at the door of the hut.
'In six days your daughter will be twenty,' he said, 'and I shall come to claim her as my wife.'

Black Thorn knew what he must do. He called his daughter and the young Indian to him and explained everything to them.
'I'm sorry,' he said. 'I know how you feel and I, too, would not wish to see my only daughter as the wife of a spirit. But what can I do? I cannot break my word. It is only because of the Sea Spirit that Thorn Flower has become what she is. From him she has learned to spin and sew and weave. I did not teach her to cook or to clean. Though she never saw him, he taught her everything she knows.'

The young man sprang to his feet. 'I shall fight for her,' he declared. 'If I lose, then that is the worse for me. But she is worth fighting for.'

On the sixth day Black Thorn took his boat out to fish as usual while the young couple waited together in the hut for the arrival of the Sea Spirit. He was fishing far out from the shore when he saw a small cloud approaching over the waves. It grew bigger and bigger as it swept over his boat, then moved to hover over the village of Pelluhue, seeming to centre itself over his own hut. Suddenly there was a great crash and a hurricane unleashed its violence on the village. The next minute Black Thorn saw a whirlwind of sand rising over the little settlement, twisting and swirling round and round, hiding the huts from view. Clinging desperately to his boat, he huddled there for hours as the wind roared and the waves tossed him violently to and fro.

At last a deep calm came and Black Thorn paddled his boat cautiously towards the land. Everything he saw was changed. The sand was piled hundreds of metres deep over the village, carved into fantastic shapes by the lashing wind. There was no sign of human life. The hut where the lovers had waited had become their tomb and the Sea Spirit had taken its terrible revenge. The village had vanished forever.

Symbols in the Central and South American myths

At the beginning of each chapter the artist has illustrated some of the objects and symbols identified with the characters and events of the stories.

p. 11 MYTHS OF THE NEW WORLD Many of the mountains of Central and South America are still active volcanoes, whose mysterious power gave rise to myths and legends all over the region. The buildings in the centre are from the ancient city of Teotihuacan in Central America and symbolize here the achievements of the great civilizations of the past.

p. 13 GODS OF THE AZTECS The head at the top is a representation of the Feathered Serpent god Quetzalcoatl, from the pyramid of Quetzalcoatl in Teotihuacan. Below is a design from a sacrificial stone used in combat sacrifices, above a stylized image of the god Huitzilopochtli (from an Aztec war drum) and the earth goddess Coatlicue (from a stone statue).

p. 30 THE MAYAS AND THEIR MYTHS The Observatory tower from the Maya city of Palenque, with characters from a Maya Codex now in the Dresden museum, and a Maya head-dress. The small designs and symbols around the border were part of a calendar system.

p. 52 THE INCAS, CHILDREN OF THE SUN The ancient city of Machu Picchu, whose buildings and terraces are perfect examples of the Incas' engineering skills. In the centre are ears of maize and llamas, symbolizing their agricultural skills. Below, is a design from a coastal tapestry which formed part of a tribute sent by conquered coastal tribes to Cuzco.

p. 74 MYTHS OF THE HIGH ANDES One of the great stone statues from Tiahuanaco, with two of the figures carved on either side of the great Gateway of the Sun.

p. 77 MYSTERIES OF THE VALLEY At the top is a pottery vessel painted with a design of a bird stealing beans, from the Nazca culture of the second or third century BC. Below, typical Nazca style animal motifs, and a section of one of the famous Nazca lines in the Atacama Desert. At the bottom is a clay bowl decorated in classic Nazca style and a Nazca animal motif.

p. 82 SPIRITS OF THE FOREST Between the bird and snake are designs based on patterns of wooden spindle whorls used by the Xingu tribes. At the bottom are two wooden dance pendants. The pointed sticks are used for digging.

p. 91 TALES FROM THE AMAZON The two parrots who married the Sun and Moon above an aerial view of the great Amazon river as it winds through thickly forested country. Below, bark masks used in ceremonial dances.

p. 99 TALES OF MISCHIEF AND MAGIC A Bororo ceremonial feather head-dress and decorative feathers. Below are Bororo arrow tips and bull-roarers, instruments which are whirled around to produce a roaring sound. The jaguar (bottom) is in many Indian stories.

p. 111 PEOPLE OF THE GREAT RIVERS Tropical American toucan and butterflies represent the abundant animal life of the jungle.

p. 119 THE FAR SOUTH The ibis, cormorants and other South Atlantic seabirds figure in many of the stories from this remote tip of South America. Snow-capped mountains and icebergs were familiar sights in the Yamana environment.

p. 125 TALES FROM THE SOUTHERN PLAINS On the plains, shelters were tent-like skin structures. Below is a Mapuche woman with Mapuche pottery, and sticks and balls used in the Mapuche version of hockey.

The sources

Alexander, H B, *The Mythology of all Races, vol XI Latin America*. Marshall Jones Company, Boston, 1920

Arguedas, J M, Bondy, C M and S S, *Ollantay y cantos y narraciones quechuas*. Ediciones Peisa, Lima 1974

Arios-Larreta, *A Literaturas abórigines de America*. Editorial Indo America, 1968

Brett, W H, *The Indian Tribes of Guiana*. Bell & Daldy, London 1868

Burland, C and Forman, W, *The Aztecs*. Orbis Publishing, London 1980

Burland, Nicholson and Osborne, *Mythology of the Americas*. Hamlyn, London 1966

Caso, A (trans. Lowell Dunham), *People of the Sun*. Norman, University of Oklahoma Press, 1958

Coe, M D, *The Maya*. Thames and Hudson, London 1966

Howard-Malverde, Rosaleen, *Dioses ey diablos: tradición de Cañar, Ecuador*. Paris, 1981

Launey, M, *Introduction à la langue et à litterature aztèques*. L'Harmattan, Paris, 1980

Larousse World Mythology. Hamlyn Publishing Group Ltd, London, 1965

Shaw, M, *Según nuestros antepasados*. Instituto Lingüístico de Verano, 1972

Spence, L, *The gods of Mexico*. T Fisher Unwin, Ltd, London, 1923
Myths of Mexico and Peru. George Harrap & Co, London, 1914

Steward, J H and Faron, L C, *Native peoples of South America*. McGraw-Hill Book Co., New York, 1959

Wilbert, J (ed), *Folk literature of the Yamana Indians*. University of California Press, Berkeley and Los Angeles, 1977

More recently collected stories have been retold from the following sources which are gratefully acknowledged:

Amerindia , 1980 'The Quarrel of the Suns' p. 29

Folklore: Revista de Cultura Tradicional Año 1 Julio 1966, no 1, Cuzco, Peru, 'Amaru Inca' p. 60

Howard-Malverde, Rosaleen, 'The snake sister' p. 61

Latin American Indian Literature, University of Pittsburg, vol I no 1, Spring 1977, 'Jokoramo the monkey' p. 110; vol 2 no 1 Spring 1978, 'The origin of salt', p. 105; vol 3 no 1 Spring 1979 'Why you must not strike children,' p. 108

Index